BEARING WITNESS TO EVIL

JON AUSTIN BURKETT   STEVEN R. NEAL

BEARING WITNESS TO EVIL

gatekeeper press™

Columbus, Ohio

Bearing Witness to Evil

Published by Gatekeeper Press
2167 Stringtown Rd, Suite 109
Columbus, OH 43123-2989
www.GatekeeperPress.com

Cover design: Louis Penn
Graphic design: Louis Penn

Although the stories in this book are based upon true occurrences, precise details may be slightly modified to protect innocent witnesses or ancillary parties.

ISBN (paperback): 9781662909542
eISBN: 9781662909559

What People are Saying About
Bearing Witness to Evil

15 crime cases that are truly dreadful. Jon Burkett, (Crime Reporter), and Steve Neal, (Lawman), give the reader first-hand accounts and insider tidbits that can only come from someone who was at the scene of the crime. The *Story Behind the Story* segments that follow each crime case highlight and honor real world heroes whose experiences are interesting, informative, and inspiring. If you like true crime stories, and real-life heroes, ***Bearing Witness to Evil*** is a must read.

Patrick Yoes – FOP National President

Steve Neal and Jon Burkett have taken the horrors of evil and death they witnessed, and with compassion, shared the stories of the victims and those left behind. In sharing the "Story Behind the Story" in each chapter, Steve and Jon have given great honor to the memory of those gone too soon. Steve and Jon are truly Warriors, Servants, Leaders – from protecting and serving their community in their respective careers, to now, sharing the stories of those who were the least, the last, and the lost, forgotten by many. Thank you for your compassion, and for Bearing Witness to Evil.

Pat Welsh – Founder and CEO of PJ Welsh and Associates, Author, Speaker, Trainer

My brother [Robert Rush] was murdered in a robbery. To lose a loved one is devastating! There is so much pain, questions of why, and then comes the anger. Jon Burkett, CBS Channel 6 news reporter, called and asked for an interview. From that point on, Jon, the police department, Steve Neal, and I became part of a team working together to solve my brother's case. Years passed, but, finally, the day came, my brother's killer was captured. Thanks Jon and Steve for assisting me in my personal mission, keeping me informed, and partnering with me in my quest for justice.

Livingston Rush - Co-victim of homicide.
Victim rights advocate

Serial Killers, Murderers, Abductors, Rapist, Bank Robbers, Sniper Terrorists, Home Invasion Burglars, Death Row Escapees, *Bearing Witness to Evil* has them all. The real-world crime stories are compelling, yet maddeningly sorrowful at the same time. I was awe-struck by the *Stories Behind the Story"* segments. Steve Neal (Lawman) and Jon Burkett (Crime Reporter) masterfully blend reverence for victims and loved ones with a fervent quest for justice.

Mike Wade- Henrico County Sheriff (Ret.)

I found *Bearing Witness to Evil* to be captivating, and thought provoking. The true crime chronicles are riveting, the *Stories Behind the Story"* inspirational. The intersection of two men from different generations and different professions collectively seeking justice on behalf of victims and survivors is uniquely intriguing. Some of the crimes are older, some quite recent, all real-life gruesomeness shared from an insider's perspective. Worthy read for any true crime buff!

Orlando Salinas – Freelance Journalist and Writer

A riveting read! Some of these stories hit close to home as I work in law enforcement in the metro Richmond area and vividly remember some of the cases and accompanying headlines. There's even one chapter in this book that details a fascinating story of one of my former bosses that I wasn't aware of until reading *Bearing Witness to Evil*. The blend of traumatic events and compassion in recalling those stories speaks volumes to the character of Steve Neal and Jon Burkett.

Sergeant Deb Oaks - Henrico Police Department

It's FANTASTIC! A real page-turner with stories behind the stories! Jon and Steve have a winner with this piece!! Shout out to Louis Penn for just an INCREDIBLE cover! Blown Away!!

Jeff Katz – Chesterfield County Chief of Police

Dedications

Public service is as noble a venture as anything known to mankind. This book is dedicated to the men and women, past and present, who selflessly give their all in the service of others. Without our everyday heroes, society would disintegrate into chaos. Jon and Steve offer a heartfelt salute to all who have served honorably as guardians of their community!

Steve

To my grandchildren: Kaylee, Bryson, Kylie, Alexander, and Avalynn,

You have been well taught, trust yourself and follow your heart. Position family first, the more that you do to help loved ones, the happier you will be. Be courageous, remain humble, and live by the spiritual teachings of God.

In all endeavors, put in the work. Maximum effort merged with integrity leads to success. Continuously improve yourself, and treat people as you would like to be treated. Fear no evil, stand firm in your beliefs, be strong.

When troubles come and your heart is burdened, know that you are deeply loved! Struggles along the way should be viewed as learning lessons. Hindsight often brings clarity, revealing that the setback was actually preparing you for something far greater. May the memory of the loving bond between us enrich you for a lifetime.

Jon

My wife, Malorie Burkett, has always encouraged me to achieve and pursue my goals no matter how outlandish and unattainable they seem. I dedicate this book to her and my children; Sophia, Austin, and Clara. I often tell them stories of tragic events that I have witnessed to warn them that evil lurks in all walks of life.

At an early age, my Mom, Dad, brothers, sisters, and both sets of grandparents, knew that I had a knack for writing and a passion for telling stories. I produced the weekly newspaper Huntwood Gazette. My future career truly came to light when I started using video to assist my storytelling as a U.S. Navy journalist.

I also dedicate this book to my colleagues at WTVR-TV a CBS affiliate in Richmond. Many of them inspire me to do good work and to be compassionate when telling stories of victims of crime. It is easy to get jaded by the evil I have seen, but understanding the human element behind the victims and their families keeps me grounded and sensitive to the topic.

Finally, I dedicate this book to Steve Neal. I first met him on a crime scene in Chesterfield County, Virginia in the early 2000's. I knew through the years that our friendship would grow and that something productive would be produced from our life experiences. **Bearing Witness to Evil** is a testament to his long hours of investigative work with the police department, and my long hours of following every detail to bring our readers the Story Behind the Story.

Acknowledgements

Facts, details, and photographs regarding the case studies in this book are a combination of law enforcement files, public court documents, WTVR channel 6 media archives, and the personal recollections and experiences of the authors.

Foreword

Prior to the 2020 protests, riots, and devastation to Richmond's world-famous Monument Avenue, this Virginia metropolis had been bearing witness to prosperity, growth, and a growing national reputation as a cool, hip, and distinctive area to work and play.

Publications across the land have listed Richmond among the nation's most vibrant, up and coming cities, a stark turnaround from the 90's, when it was simply known as a murder city. In 1994, RVA was the second deadliest city in the nation. It wasn't just the sheer number of murders, but how evil so many were. There is no other word.

Children – even babies, deliberately executed or killed by madmen running wild. Deadly sexual assaults. Whole families wiped out. Teen-aged hit men. Broad daylight massacres and gunfights in crowded neighborhoods. Innocents slaughtered as if they were in some hellish video game. But it was all too real.

Rva's long-standing poverty, gang and segregation problems had boiled over. It was like each criminal was striving to be the most callous, the most evil. One murdered a stranger seconds after midnight struck on New Year's Eve simply because he wanted to be the first killer of the year.

Just as RVA's hot, ugly history sprouted a wild art and music scene known around the world, it spurred a devilish outrageous criminal culture that made national headlines all-too often. The city's main streets almost completely shut down. White and black residents and business-owners fled. Except for its growing university, the city was largely a ghost town.

As a reporter of 32-years for the Richmond-Times Dispatch and then CBS-6, I had a front-row seat for all of it. So did CBS-6's Jon Burkett and Chesterfield Police veteran Steve Neal.

I had known Jon for years, but I really got to know him while reporting on the New Year's Day massacre in 2006. Even though we were competitors, Jon and I worked together to gather the threads to this slaughter and that of another family a few days later. No other reporter has sources like Jon. Few work as tirelessly as Jon or Steve. They have more of one thing that many try hard not to lose when they are immersed in violent tragedies. *Heart.*

Steve and Jon feel these crimes. I've seen Jon in tears, totally devastated. When they go to a family who has been gutted by tragedy, the family can see the heart, the love. Again, and again, other reporters would say "How did Jon get that interview?" Or, they'd be asked by editors and producers 'How did Jon scoop them again."

It is so easy to be shocked and alarmed by a horrible crime. It is also easy to block it out, to let it fade, because there is always another one, isn't there? And, after all, it didn't happen to you. It is easy to miss the aftermath the investigations, trials, and the lingering pain and depression of the survivors.

The lessons we can learn. Jon and Steve haven't forgotten, they still feel them. Steve and Jon are the perfect partners to bring us the behind-the-scenes aftermaths of Richmond's most troubling crimes.

This southern town has a history of evil: it was a slave market capital; capital of the Confederacy; capital of segregation and concentrated poverty. Capital of failed schools, illegitimacy, illiteracy, and yes, murder and mayhem. These chapters from Jon and Steve may be ugly, but they are real! That is fitting, because for all of its evil history, Richmond is as real as it gets.

Mark Holmberg 2003 Pulitzer Prize nominee as a Times-Dispatch columnist, retired CBS-6 commentator

Preface

"Thou Shall Not Kill." There is no ambiguity in the sixth commandment, yet historical evidence makes it clear that a long line of murderers have inhabited the earth since the beginning of time. The famous biblical story of Cain and Abel details the first known homicide, an illicit death perpetrated by a jealous sibling. Today, as in the past, the unlawful killing of one person by another remains a calamity upon both our spirit and our soul.

Sadly, Richmond, Virginia (RVA) has not been immune to the bloody shortcomings of man. From the indigenous Native Americans, to Henricus colonists, to current-day residents, we are forced to grapple with the scourge of unlawfully spilled blood running in our streets. RVA, though no different from other major metropolitan regions, knows all too well the loss of mortal capital steadily draining the essence and spirit of our human existence.

Headlines from long-standing accounts demonstrate evil motives have remained consistent throughout time. Sex, power, greed, revenge, or jealousy can be found in nearly all of the criminal killings in our history. Arguments, fights, and robberies have also historically played a significant role in RVA's murderous landscape. By 1994, guns, drugs, and gangs catapulted Richmond, Virginia into the dubious distinction of being the second deadliest city - per capita – IN THE NATION.

For more than 35-years, Steve Neal (Lawman) & Jon Burkett (Crime Reporter) have had a front-row seat to blood, guts, and tears in RVA. We have sampled the fear, horror, and terror found in our midst. Jon and Steve have a personal connection to each of the cases detailed in this book. The pages that follow will take you behind the crime scene tape for a peek into some of the Capital City's most infamous criminal incidents.

Our featured narratives were not chosen because they are all inclusive of our professional experiences, but instead, they are showcased because the circumstances of the cases were enormously impactful. The *"Story Behind the Story"* segment that follows each crime case exposes fascinating backstage details, and highlights heroic behavior from everyday citizens who never planned on becoming a witness to evil.

Prepare to swallow the lump in your throat as you enter our world. Along the way, be careful not to contaminate evidence by stepping in a pool of wet blood. The emotional heartache and suffering that you are about to encounter will very likely bring tears to your eyes. If you listen intently, *like us*, you may hear blameless victims screaming out for justice!

Table of Contents

Prologue

For the Dead and the Living, We Must Bear Witness

Elie Wiesel was a Nobel prize winning writer and activist. His much-admired memoir, **Night**, described his experiences surviving the Holocaust. In 1978, Wiesel was appointed as chair of the President's Commission on the Holocaust. While working on this project, Wiesel famously said "For the dead and the living, we must bear witness."

Elie Wiesel's well-regarded words are engraved in stone at the entrance to the United States Holocaust Museum. In his dedication speech, Wiesel said "For not only are we responsible for the memories of the dead, we are also responsible for what we are doing with those memories."

This introduction will help our readers understand why your authors gravitated toward our chosen professions. The Crime Reporter and the Lawman have dedicated ourselves to being much more than just empathetic observers. In our work, we encounter the vicarious trauma that invades the world of the criminally wounded. For us, *Bearing Witness* means that we vow to compassionately apply our core beliefs while on the job.

Call to Action

Legendary author Leo Tolstoy once said "When the suffering of another creature causes you to feel pain, come as close as you can to him who suffers, and try to help him." Reassuring those who are hurting, ignites a fire that fuels our intrinsic motivation.

Performing our jobs in the most impactful way drives our behavior. Ensuring that our actions make a difference in the lives of those in need leads to self-satisfaction.

We see tears fall and hearts break. The gut-wrenching pain and concern that is felt deep in our soul arouses a call to kindhearted engagement on behalf of victims. With our words, and our acts, we fight for justice for those who are incapacitated. A caring comment, a hug, and diligent work on behalf of the grief-stricken are valuable ways to respect the living, and the dead.

Witnessing and Testimony

Witness, witnessing, and testimony are terms with multi-layered meaning. The eyes of the Lawman and the Crime Reporter have witnessed both kindness and cruelty. The aforementioned Elie Wiesel teaches us that "To listen to a witness, is to become a witness." In addition to what we see and hear, Jon and Steve witness by sharing heartfelt principles.

Most days we testify, or witness by life example. Personal testimony via words, deeds, and modeling offers us a spiritual grace that facilitates the refinement of our souls. Value driven witnessing allows us to connect sympathetically with other people, and experience a feeling of worthiness.

Honoring Survivors

Humility reminds us that pain and loss are the constant companions of the surviving family members of crime victims. These innocent co-victims have told us repetitively that, for them, it doesn't matter how many years pass. When they "Walk down a street, sit in a room, hear a voice, or see someone who looks like their loved one, it never goes away."

Evil, especially when directed toward the blameless, is horrific and flagrantly unfair. Survivors carry a burden that no-one should have to endure. Dr. Diane Langberg (recognized globally for 45-years of clinical work with trauma victims) notes "Trauma has a profound spiritual impact.... It mutilates hope; it shatters faith; it turns the world upside down." As Steve and Jon listen empathetically, we *Bear Witness* to those who are left behind. Each and every time, we strive to confer dignity, safety, and comfort upon the survivors.

Those who work in responder professions are secondary witnesses to trauma. As we help survivors deal with their suffering, we are honoring their loved ones by *Bearing Witness* to anguish. This aspect of assistance is a ministry of sorts, offering the injured an opportunity to let go of some of their emotional burden. As we strive to be elite performers, we ensure that empathetic interaction is a high priority in carrying out our professional responsibilities.

Bearing Witness as a Form of Service

The Merriam Webster Dictionary says that service, "Involves an act rendered in the public interest; a helpful act; to volunteer in the community; to make a difference." Labor union leader Walter Reuther proclaimed that "There is no greater calling than to serve your fellow men. There is no greater contribution than to help the weak. There is no greater satisfaction than to have done it well."

Jon and Steve think of *Bearing Witness* as compassionate aid. Our intentions are charitable, our gentleness must be transparent. Our tolerance and generosity should be easily recognizable. Author, speaker, and marketing consultant Michael Port says that "We are in the business of serving other people as you stand in the service of your destiny and express yourself through your work." The remnants of *our work, our service,* defines *our* personal legacy.

Relentless Perseverance

In the earliest form of the English language, the term evil meant anything that was bad, vicious, or cruel. As a Crime Reporter and a Lawman, our jobs frequently place us in the position of witnessing evil. We have seen things that cannot be removed from our collective psyche. Our experiences have changed us, and not always for the better. Yet, we continue to doggedly return to the battlefield.

Bearing Witness cannot prevent dreadful events from occurring, but it can empower us to inspire transformative hopefulness. Amidst all the carnage, humanity must continue to nourish the spirit with positive thoughts, never forgetting that there must always be enthusiasm and passion for the future.

Hope

As allies against evil, the Lawman and the Crime Reporter strive to leave this world a better place. The wise amongst us understand that doing good things for others offers a roadmap to happiness and contentment. We encourage our readers to treat everyone they meet as if they matter. As you walk beside us through the pages of this book, know that it is our sincere desire that all who have been wounded by unlawful criminal behavior are blessed by abundant mercy.

CHAPTER 1

New Year's Nightmare

RICHMOND, VA, *January 1, 2006, Steve Neal and Jon Burkett remember the case well.*

January 1, 2006

A city resident went to a friend's house in Woodland Heights on New Year's Day. His intention was to inquire if his friend needed help preparing for a party that was planned for later that day. When the man arrived, he thought that it was odd that the front door to the home was open. He stepped onto the porch and saw smoke coming from the residence. The friend immediately called 911.

Soon, the City of Richmond Fire and Emergency Services Department arrived and started working the fire. What they were about to discover shocked and horrified even the grisliest public safety professional. In the basement of the house at Chesterfield and West 31st street, firefighters began to discover dead bodies. One by one, the firefighters removed the bodies from the smoldering house.

It quickly became apparent that the bodies found dead in the basement were those of an entire family. The deceased were Bryan Harvey, his wife Katherine Harvey, and their daughters Stella, 9, and Ruby, 4. Bryan Harvey 49, was a Henrico School employee and the lead singer/guitarist of the rock band House of Freaks. Kathy Harvey 39, was the co-owner of a popular local toy shop called

World of Mirth in Richmond's Carytown district.

The bodies of the Harvey family had been grotesquely ill-treated. The adults had severe blunt force trauma (from a claw hammer) to the head. Their throats had been cut, and they were bound with electrical cord and tape. The children had died of smoke inhalation, but they had also suffered blunt-force trauma and stab wounds in the back.

During their investigation, police discovered that jewelry, a small amount of cash, and other miscellaneous items were missing from the home.

Potential for Additional Victims

The police investigation into the Harvey murder took several unusual twists and turns. One of the most bizarre of these peculiarities was that this crime was eerily but unknowingly interrupted. Nine-year-old Stella Harvey had enjoyed a sleepover with a friend on New Year's Eve. The mother of Stella's friend brought her home sometime after 9 a.m. on New Year's Day. None of the three new arrivals to the home had any way of knowing that the killers were actually in the house at that very moment. More details of this encounter will be found in the *Story Behind the Story* segment that follows this report.

January 3, 2006 - Home Invasion in Chesterfield County, Virginia

Chesterfield County Police responded to investigate a home invasion robbery. A couple who lived on Hollywood Drive reported that they had been robbed by two men and a woman. The suspects had gained entry into the home by pretending to ask for directions.

The robbers made it clear that it was their intention to gag and bind the victims with duct tape before burning the house to the ground. The husband pointed out that his wife was severely disabled and desperately needed his help. He pleaded with the offenders, begging them not to tie his family up. For whatever reason, the killers went along with the plea, and ultimately did not secure these victims with the duct tape, nor did they set the home ablaze.

The suspects stole numerous items from the home including a computer, a television, and hundreds of dollars in cash. The victims told police that the female home invasion suspect looked familiar, and that she was possibly an associate of a victim family member. Police located and interviewed the relative. Ashly Baskerville and her two male associates, (Ray Dandridge and Cooley Gray) were identified as probable offenders.

Physical evidence was recovered at the scene. After their initial investigation, Chesterfield Police strongly suspected that their home invasion suspects were likely also involved in the Harvey home invasion and murder. Chesterfield Police contacted Richmond Police and provided suspect information to their law enforcement neighbors.

Though unknown to law enforcement at the time, investigation later revealed that Ray and Cooley had been couch-surfing with a family at an apartment complex that is within walking distance of this Chesterfield crime scene.

Seven Dead in a Seven-Day Time Period

January, 6 2006, Check the Welfare of the Baskerville Family

It has been reported publicly that Ashly Baskerville was a troubled person nearly all of her life. Family members have said that

(RICHMOND TIMES-DISPATCH/AP)

by the time she was 10, she was hanging out with a bad crowd. When she was 12, her mother and step-father turned her over to the Department of Social Services. Ashly spent much of her teenage years in shelters and treatment programs. Baskerville was locked up just two months after her 18th birthday.

After receiving a phone call from the mother of an Ashly friend, homicide Detectives knew that it was time to have a chat with the problematic young woman. When police responded to the Baskerville house on East Broad Rock Road in the Swansboro neighborhood, it became clear that something was very wrong. Soon, there was more than enough suspicion to force entry into the residence. Once inside, police found a crime scene so vile and disgusting that it physically sickened some of the first responders.

For the second time in less than a week, Richmond Police had

(RICHMOND TIMES-DISPATCH/AP)

discovered a family dead in their own home. The Baskerville family had been gagged, and bound with tape. The mother and step-father had their throats slashed. All three victims had suffocated due to the layers of duct tape wrapped around their heads. The adult daughter had a plastic bag wrapped around her head as well, secured with duct tape.

The male victim was Percyell Tucker, 56, who worked as a forklift driver. He liked to make pies as a hobby. The older female was Mary Baskerville-Tucker, 46, who worked at a laundry business and liked to visit the elderly with members of her church. The younger female victim was; yes, you guessed it, problematic female suspect, Ashly Baskerville. When found dead, Ashly Baskerville was wearing the wedding ring of prior victim Bryan Harvey.

The Tucker-Baskerville home had been ransacked. Mr. Tucker's green Chevrolet Blazer was stolen, loaded with electronics and bags stuffed with items from the burglary.

Police learned thru investigation that Ashly Baskerville had developed a relationship with an inmate based on a profile posted on a Web site for prison pen pals. The name of this inmate was Ray Dandridge. Police also confirmed that Ashly and Dandridge were recently in the company of Dandridge's nephew, longtime criminal Ricky "Cooley" Gray. A BOL (Be on the Lookout) was issued for the suspects and the stolen vehicle. The hunt for the pair of brutal killers was on.

Arrest of Ray Dandridge and Ricky Gray

Investigative leads led police to Philadelphia, Pennsylvania. On January 7, 2006 a heavily armed SWAT team stormed the home of Ray Dandridge's father. Dandridge surrendered without a fight.

When located hiding behind a water heater, Ricky Gray decided to engage with the police. A struggle ensued, but Ricky Gray quickly lost the battle. He was pepper sprayed with Oleoresin Capsicum. Gray ended up with numerous bruises and received stitches to close a wound on his head.

Confessions of Ray Dandridge and Ricky Gray

Ray Joseph Dandridge had been released from prison approximately 2-months before the Harvey family murders. Nicknamed "the terminator," Dandridge had served more than ten years for armed robbery. He quickly confessed to his involvement in the Baskerville killings. According to court transcripts, he insinuated that he had grown tired of short-term girlfriend Ashly Baskerville, and that she was "In the way."

Trial testimony included that Dandridge advised that he had been at the Harvey murders, and that Ashly Baskerville had served as the lookout and getaway driver. Dandridge reportedly said that the group had been cruising the neighborhood looking for homes to burglarize. Dandridge said that the Harvey home had been chosen at random, simply because the front door was open. Ray Dandridge denied personal involvement in the killing of the Harveys.

Ricky Javon Gray provided a detailed, three-page written

confession in which he described using a kitchen knife and claw hammer to kill the Harveys. Gray would later testify that their "Screams were shrill, indicative of the hell they were enduring." Gray said that Dandridge beat the final breath out of Bryan, Kathryn, Stella and Ruby Harvey with a ballpeen hammer.

Gray's Timberland boots, taken from the Philadelphia arrest site, had the blood of Bryan and Stella Harvey on them as confirmed thru DNA testing. Gray told police that he was high on PCP when he killed the Harvey family.

Authorities subsequently connected Gray and Dandridge to a New Year's Eve throat-slashing attack on an Arlington, Virginia man. Gray also confessed to killing his wife Treva Gray in 2005.

Sentence for Ricky Gray and Ray Dandridge

Ray Dandridge pleaded guilty to 3 counts of Capital Murder and received multiple life sentences without the possibility of parole. Ray Joseph Dandridge, Inmate # 1159354 is incarcerated at the Keen Mountain Correctional Center in Oakwood, Virginia.

A jury needed only 30-minutes to find Ricky Gray guilty of multiple counts of capital murder. A psychologist testified that Gray came from a family filled with alcoholism, substance abuse, and sexual abuse. Even after hearing this mitigating testimony, the jury sentenced him to death.

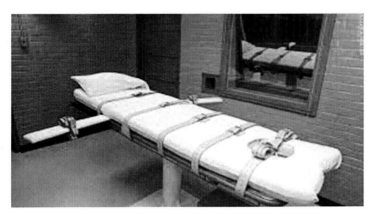

After a little more than 8-years, Ricky Gray exhausted all of his appeals. He was executed on January 18, 2017, at 9:42 PM by lethal injection at Greenville Correctional Center

Story Behind The Story

She Saved Us

"This is my commandment, that you love one another, even as I have loved you. Greater love has no one than this…. that someone lays down their life for their friends." It's a bible passage from the book of John, usually heard at funerals for fallen police officers, firefighters, or military personnel. However, it also pertains to people that possess the extraordinary quality of compassion and love for mankind. It was a bible verse on full display the morning of January 1, 2006 in South Richmond, Virginia.

Birthday Party for the Girls

Just hours from their annual New Year's Day tradition, Kirsten Perkinson had picked up a group of cackling and boisterous eight-year-old girls from an overnight slumber party in Oregon Hill. Loaded up in a minivan, Perkinson was making her rounds, dropping the girls off at their respective homes until it was down to just two left.

The girls, Perkinson's daughter, and 9-year-old Stella Harvey, were the closest of friends who only lived two blocks from each other on the city's south side. The giggly girls were in the back seat of the minivan, recalls Perkinson. They were rapping and reciting lyrics to "Apple Bottom Jeans" a hit song at the time from Flo-Rida. Perkinson smiles as she tells the story 14-years later, adding that she vividly remembers telling the girls they were going to get her in trouble with Stella's parents. Stella Harvey laughed and said something like "Ms. Kirsten, my mom won't get mad at you because you are so nice, the most lovable. We'll take care of you," said Stella.

Arrival at the Harvey Home

Both Stella and Perkinson's daughter would beg Kirsten to spend more time with each other as the minivan rolled closer and closer to Chesterfield and West 31st Street. The minivan came to a stop in front of the Harvey house. Before Perkinson had time to take the keys out of the ignition, the two little girls had pulled back the slide side door and made a bee-line to the front door of Stella's home.

Kirsten vividly remembers the sequence of events. She said "We walked up the front walkway. The front door was open." Stella Harvey pulled open the screen door and burst into the entryway and yelled HELLO as was her normal pattern. There was no response. HELLO, she said again. Still silence. Kirsten told the girls "Maybe they went out to get some stuff for the party." She then said to Stella; "We will be back shortly for the party anyway, why don't you go home with us, we'll leave a note." At that moment, Kathy Harvey came running up the stairs and threw the basement door open.

Conversation with Kathy Harvey

As soon as she threw the door open, Kirsten said, "I asked her, honey, what's the matter?" Kirsten told us that "We had all had the stomach flu, her face was white as a sheet. She made like a gun with her hand, and made a circular motion with her finger." Kathy stated "Everything is really crazy." Kirsten thought that Kathy was stressing over the impending party. Kirsten said, "That's okay, do you want me to come over a little early, bring food, make the house smell good? We can put collards on the stove."

At this point Kathy was one step down on the basement stairway. Stella went to her mom on the stairwell. Kathy kissed Stella on top of her head and let her walk down the stairs toward the basement. Kirsten's daughter tried to follow her friend Stella downstairs. Kathy stopped her, motioning as if to say, just stay there. The disappointed young friend crossed her arms and dropped her chin to her chest.

Kirsten recalls that the encounter was odd. While her daughter was against Kathy Harvey's body, the young girl momentarily stood and looked down the stairs. The child did not follow Stella, and she did not say a thing. Kirsten empathetically said to Kathy; "I love you; I'll see you. We'll come back early, don't worry about anything." The last thing that Kathy Harvey said was "That would be good." Kathy then turned around and went back down stairs.

Kirsten Perkinson said that while still in the Harvey house, she looked at her daughter and said "That is really weird." Her daughter felt the vibes too, saying "I know." Kirsten asked her daughter, "What did she say?' The younger of the two replied "She said that she wasn't feeling well." Kirsten asked her daughter, where are Bryan and Ruby? The young girl said that they were downstairs.

"It kind of satisfied me," said Kirsten. The Perkinson's left the Harvey home that morning without knowing, *that at that very moment*, dangerous killers were holding the family hostage. Moments later, the entire Harvey family would be dead.

Am I Being Paranoid?

Kirsten said that "I turned around, I felt I little hurt, because I felt like she wanted me to leave." Kirsten, a family friend for almost two decades, knew that Kathryn had the tendency to keep things short and sweet, especially if she was feeling stressed. "I was okay with it; it was her business-like personality. She had been working like a dog at her toy shop over the Christmas season."

Kirsten and her daughter got in their car and went home. When she arrived home, Kirsten said to her husband "That was really weird. Sometimes I think I imagine things, and I think I'm just too sensitive or paranoid." When her husband asked why she would say that, Kirsten said "Well, she [Kathy] was kind of holding me at arm's length. I felt like she wanted me to leave, I don't know why she was being so frosty towards me." Her husband said, "Oh honey, you're just imagining things. Don't worry, they probably had an argument or something, you know how it is when you're having a party."

The House is on Fire

When Kirsten got home, she and her husband continued prepping food for the party. It wasn't long before friends were calling frantically. Thick black smoke was billowing out the basement of the Harvey home. Kirsten's husband ran to the Harvey house, only to return a short time later with horrific news. He was breathing heavy and shouted, "They're all gone!" Kirsten says her heart sank as the words left his lips in what seemed like slow motion.

Trembling with sadness and fear, Kirsten felt the need to go to the Harvey home to see for herself. Crime tape was draped around the property. There was a flurry of activity by firefighters and police detectives.

It was a Tough Day

After the Harvey family was found dead, Kirsten Perkinson and many of her friends spent the entire day at the police station. Kirsten was the last person known to have seen them alive. The close male friend who actually reported the fire was considered a potential suspect.

Detective Joseph Fultz, from the Richmond Police Department, pulled Kirsten aside. Perkinson knew then that she would endure hours and hours of questions and most likely learn gruesome details of her friends' deaths. She made it clear to Jon and Steve that she has enormous respect for Detective Fultz. "He was like an angel, he protected me throughout the entire thing. I was completely cocooned by Joe Fultz. He was the only person that dealt with me."

Are my Daughter and I in Danger?

The days that followed brought great fear and anxiety to Kirsten and her family. Since suspects in the Harvey murder were unknown, she feared that she might be next. "While we waited for the investigation to progress, I was afraid that they [bad guys] would be coming for me and my daughter," she said.

Perkinson remembers thinking that a stalker man that lived close to her might be the killer. She also knew that Kathryn Harvey had recently rekindled a relationship with an estranged sister. Kathryn had been helping her sister deal with an allegedly abusive husband. The husband was military special forces. Did he learn of Kathryn's help and retaliate against the Harvey family?

And, Richmond police took a very hard look at a man who was a close friend of the family. In addition to being a musician in Bryan Harvey's band, he was also the person to discover the Harvey house on fire. Perkinson said she knew instantly that this long-time family friend wasn't involved.

It wasn't until the trial, where Perkinson would learn that the Harvey family was just a random target. The beloved family of four had been violently taken at the hands of three psychopathic *stranger* killers.

Special People

Kirsten said that she wished that everyone could have known the Harvey family while they were alive. "I want everyone to know that they were great people, adorable, and funny. They were the life of a party." The circle of friends had regular get-togethers, even going to the beach as a group. "Food, music, everybody singing. Really fun, smart, sharp people. They were larger than life," said Kirsten.

Forest Hill Park is a place that the Harvey family loved to visit. A 2-ton granite marker on the north side of a bridge features a bronze plaque with an inscription memorializing the Harvey family and a self-taken family portrait cast in bronze relief. Nearly 200 people attended its unveiling.

Aftermath of the Massacre

Kirsten Perkinson says she has spent a lot of time analyzing and thinking about what she could've done differently. She's gone through periods of blaming herself as to why she didn't recognize the signs, if Kathryn was indeed giving them. "I wish I had known something," Kirsten said. "There was no way that I would have ever thought anything like that. I think she was afraid; I know that she made some tough decisions."

Nearly a decade and a half has passed since that terrifying New Year's Day. The tightknit group of friends that would gather religiously at each other's homes have scattered. Many of the families that once partied together and jammed to Bryan Harvey's music are broken. Though some are certainly thriving, others are beset by divorce, alcoholism, post-traumatic stress, and behavioral issues. "It just killed me, I'm so sorry, I can't imagine what the kids went through," said Kirsten.

A couple of years ago, a close friend helped to relieve some of Kirsten's self-imposed burden. This friend said "She was with you, for her to see your face.... You told her that you loved her." At the time, Perkinson had no idea that the words "I love you," to Kathryn as she stood in the basement door would be the last she uttered to her long-time friend.

Kirsten also wonders what her daughter may have seen as she stood side by side with Stella and Kathryn at the top of the basement steps. She has never asked her if she saw anything - while it's assumed, she may have seen the reflection of one of the killers.

Kirsten says Kathryn was an angel on earth and followed that mantra until her very last breath. Kirsten's heart is heavy that she couldn't save Kathryn or the rest of the Harvey family, but she now realizes "I may not have been able to save their lives, but she saved ours."

CHAPTER 2

Bank Insecurity

RICHMOND, VA, 1999, *Jon Burkett and Steve Neal know the case well.*

Bon Air Branch of NationsBank in Chesterfield County

Local and Federal Police were investigating a series of unrelated bank robberies in the Bon Air area of Chesterfield County, Virginia. On January 19, 1999, two men entered the Nations-Bank on Buford Road with a sawed-off shotgun. The men threatened the bank employees  with the weapon and demanded money. It was later disclosed that the robbers had taken more than $60,000 in cash. There was no security guard at this bank at that time.

Convicted Felon on Probation Hanging Out in Henrico County

A man and his girlfriend were staying at a local motel in suburban Henrico County, Virginia. They were leading a lifestyle of drug

use and drug dealing. On January 30, 1999, the hotel received noise complaints regarding the couple fighting over a shotgun. When Henrico police answered the call, the male was belligerent and refused to comply with the police officer's instructions. He was arrested for obstruction of justice.

According to court testimony, during the booking process, the man falsely told police and sheriff's deputies that his name was James Cromer. Court transcripts indicate that a friend, Cliff Sauer, helped bail him out of jail. Sauer, initially believing he was assisting Cromer, arranged bond with a bail bondsman. It was later learned that the fake James Cromer had "sawed off" the barrel of a shotgun the night before the first NationsBank robbery.

No Source of Legitimate Income

Unknown to police at the time, the fake James Cromer was really a man who was already on probation for prior convictions that included possession of marijuana with intent to distribute, receiving stolen property, and unlawful possession of a firearm by a convicted felon. Court records indicate that Cliff Sauer knew the man's real identity, and he knew that the suspect was not gainfully employed. Sauer also saw that the man had a LOT of money. Sauer is alleged to have helped the man purchase an automobile. While negotiating a "cash" deal for the automobile, Sauer is said to have asked his associate where he had obtained the funds for the purchase. The man allegedly told Sauer that he had robbed a bank. Sauer made no attempt to contact the police with this information.

2nd *Robbery of NationsBank in Bon Air*

NationsBank and several of their peer institutions determined that due to the rash of robberies in the area, they needed additional security. The Bank decided that an armed security guard posted outside the bank would be a deterrent to criminals, and provide comfort to customers and employees. They contacted a private security company who supplied one of their officers to work in uniform to fulfill the NationsBank request.

At approximately 1:00 p.m. on February 17, 1999, armed security guard Shelton Earl Dunning was posted outside the NationsBank. Dunning held the door for a male who entered the bank wearing dark sunglasses and a bulky jacket. Dunning then entered the bank directly behind this man. Based upon Dunning's actions, there is little doubt that the man's appearance and actions raised the suspicions of the on-duty guard.

According to witnesses, the man stood in the teller line behind several customers. He kept his head lowered and appeared to scan the interior of the bank. Suddenly, the man left his place in line and walked toward the security guard. Bank employees noted that the killer was within a foot or two of the guard when two gunshots reverberated throughout the building. The bleeding guard fell to the floor.

Court records and bank photographs show that the suspect was brandishing a .45 caliber handgun, approaching the tellers screaming "Money, give me money" and "If I don't get money, I'm going to kill everybody." The robber was holding a black plastic bag. Tellers advised that the robbery suspect told them something to the effect of "You have 10-seconds to give me more money."

The robber then started counting backwards from ten-to-one. The bank employees gave him all the money as quickly as they could. The man fled the bank with more than $36,000.

Security guard Dunning was killed as a result of a gunshot wound to his torso. The bullet entered the right side of Dunning's chest, causing significant injuries to his aorta. He was dead on scene when emergency services personnel arrived. Dunning's firearm never left its holster, remaining strapped securely by his side. More details involving security guard Dunning can be found in the *Story Behind the Story* segment that follows this report.

John Yancey Schmitt

The bank's 11 surveillance cameras recorded photographs of the robbery suspect approaching the teller counter, holding a bag and pointing a gun. The cameras did not however record the actual shooting of the guard. Chesterfield Police identified John Yancey Schmitt as the murder suspect after reviewing the images taken by the bank's security camera system. Four different bank employees identified Schmitt as the suspect by picking him from a photo lineup.

During the investigation, police learned of Schmitt's association with Cliff Sauer. They then discovered the Sauer connection with the man and the shotgun in the Henrico motel a couple of weeks earlier. Police located Sauer and pressured him to come clean. Court transcripts indicate that Sauer agreed to cooperate. After making a recorded phone call, Sauer and law enforcement learned that Schmitt was registered at a Williamsburg, Virginia motel under the name R. Napier. Schmitt had paid cash for a 3-day stay. He had changed the color of his hair, and purchased new clothes.

With the SWAT team in position, a tactical team crisis negotiator from James City County, Virginia, made contact with Schmitt in his motel room. His refusal to surrender began a 4-hour standoff with police. Finally, at 10:30 a.m. the following morning, nearly 3-days since the bank robbery murder in Chesterfield, Schmitt surrendered and was taken into custody.

Additional Evidence

Police obtained a search warrant for Schmitt's hotel room. Court transcripts indicate that a black bag, a .45 caliber handgun, a box of shotgun shells, a black leather jacket, and a variety of newly purchased clothing items were seized. Inside the bag was more than $27,000 in cash. Much of the recovered money had "bank bands" identifying the cash as coming from the Bon Air NationsBank.

At trial, a firearms expert testified that he had examined the handgun found in Schmitt's hotel room and the cartridge casings and bullets found in the bank. He stated that based on his examination, the cartridge casings and fatal bullets had been fired from the handgun recovered in Schmitt's room.

Conviction, Sentence, and Execution

John Yancey Schmitt claimed that he did not intend to shoot or kill the security guard. He explained that there was a fight and that the gun went off when the security guard grabbed his gun. He said that the shooting of Dunning was purely unintentional. A Chesterfield jury did not buy Schmitt's excuse, and convicted

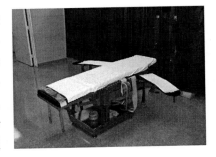

him of Capital Murder, Use of Firearm in the Commission of a Felony, and Bank Robbery. Schmitt was sentenced to death. They also gave him an additional 118-year prison sentence. According to court transcripts, Schmitt, 26, hung his head and stared at the floor as he listened impassively to the jury's verdict.

John Yancey Schmitt was executed by lethal injection at Greensville Correctional Center at Jarratt, Virginia on November 9, 2006.

Story Behind The Story

Workplace Violence

Following completion of her college degree, Richmond native Sarah Orr took a management position with NationsBank. Early in her career, she was working in Chesapeake, Virginia as a Banking Center Manager. It didn't take long for Sarah to realize that she wanted to come home. She requested, and received a transfer to the NationsBank branch in Bon Air. Sarah, who grew up in the area, knew many of the customers as long-time personal friends.

January 19th Robbery at NationsBank

Martin Luther King Day was observed on a Monday in 1999. Tuesday, after a Monday holiday, is a very busy time for the banking industry. Midmorning, Sarah Orr was sitting with her back to the door, conducting business with a loan officer. She saw the loan officers' eyes get big, then she saw the loan officer pushing buttons. Sarah immediately knew what was happening.

When she turned to look, Sarah saw two (2) men covered with hoods, masks and gloves. She saw that at least one of the men was brandishing a sawed-off shotgun. The men went to the teller window and demanded money at gunpoint. Bank employees performed flawlessly. The robbers got the money and left. No-one was hurt.

Results of the Robbery

NationsBank instantaneously showed concern for their employees. They knew that everyone at the branch was on edge. Several bank employees were shaken so badly that they never returned to work. In fact, one teenage female employee was on day #1 of her first job ever. Imagine being feet away and feeling threatened during a robbery on the first day of your working career.

Corporate officials immediately contacted private security firm Wackenhut. The armed security guard who arrived the next business day was put in place indefinitely. As her comfort level slowly increased, Sarah Orr remembers thinking "It won't happen again – lightning doesn't strike twice, I've had mine."

The Armed Security Guard

Wackenhut assigned Shelton Earl Dunning to work at the NationsBank. Prior to working for the private security firm, Shelton had recently retired from the U. S. Army with more than 20-years of service. He had 3 children, and he was engaged to be married.

Sarah Orr fondly recalls Shelton as a "big guy" who was very friendly. "He was fun loving, and he made us very comfortable," said Sarah. "He was as much business as he was fun. He was one of our teammates. We celebrated a birthday; he celebrated a birthday. We had lunch, he had lunch" Sarah said.

He would stand outside with his hat pulled down, he looked very intimidating. He was not Paul Blart, Sarah said respectfully. "We felt very comfortable while he was there. Certainly, who is going to walk past him and do something that they shouldn't do" said Sarah.

You Need Order

The break room at NationsBank was typically messy. It was not uncommon to find crumbs, trash, drinks, and utensils lying around. As in most workplaces, the refrigerator was often in less than perfect condition as well. It was easy to find old food, expired condiments, and disarray in the icebox.

Sarah Orr warmly relayed the story that follows as one example of how Shelton Dunning impacted everyone at the bank:

"Shortly after Shelton arrived, he went back to the break room. He was gone for a while. A little while later he approached and said, Come here." Sarah Orr went into the breakroom and it was clean! "Spotless, it was great" she said.

Shelton said to Sarah; "Whenever you go through a traumatic experience, like you all have gone through, you need order. It is going to help you heal, and help you feel better. This is what I could do for you!"

2nd *Robbery*

On this day, security guard Shelton Dunning's car wasn't in the parking lot when Sarah arrived for work. It was his normal practice to ensure everything was in order prior to escorting the employees into the bank. Soon, Dunning's supervisor arrived and indicated that Shelton would be running late. The supervisor indicated that Shelton had gotten part way to work, only to realize that he didn't have his gun. The guard went back home, picked up his firearm, and arrived approximately 45-minutes late.

Due to short staffing, Sarah Orr was running a teller window. In walked John Yancy Schmitt. Sarah noticed that the man was wearing sunglasses, and remembers thinking it was kind of odd. Otherwise, she had no real reason to think there was anything unusual. She remembers that there were one or two people standing in the teller line, and that he [Schmitt] got in line.

Security guard Shelton walked in behind Schmitt. Shelton stood at the back of the teller line. Sarah Orr said "Next thing I know, he ran over to Shelton, shot him point blank. Shelton didn't even have time to get his gun out of his holster." Sarah said that "The instant I heard gunshots, I thought, I might not make

28

it out of this." She further recalled that "After he shot Shelton, he came to the teller window where I was working. He held the gun sideways; I remember thinking OMG!"

Schmitt yelled, "Get down, get down. We all dropped to the floor. He demanded cash, so I just started putting everything in that bag. He kept saying more, I want more." Sarah said that she went from window to window getting what she could, throwing it in the bag. She also recalled momentarily thinking that Schmitt was going to take her new engagement ring. Quickly her thoughts turned to "*I might not live through this*; he can have my ring."

Aftermath of the Shooting

Though clearly in shock, Sarah said that "Training had prepared me, it kicked in." She instructed fellow workers to call 911. Sarah vividly recalled how she had to step over Shelton's body to lock the front door. She also remembered that she yelled "Hang on, hang on" to Shelton as she did her duty in the aftermath of the shooting. One teller went and sat with Shelton and held his hand.

Just moments after the killing and prior to police arrival, Sarah Orr saw some media person with a camera in the front parking lot. Almost at the same instant, she heard sirens and saw her mother across the street in the shopping center. Her mother was sprinting towards the bank. Sarah said "She had been getting her hair cut, heard sirens, saw the person with the camera, and started running."

"I left the bank. I saw my mom, and I had just witnessed a murder. I was 26 at the time," Sarah said. She remembers telling her mother "They killed him, they killed him. That person with the video camera was up in my grill."

Impact of the Trauma

Sarah Orr is one tough lady. She faced trauma at a level few civilian employees will ever know. She candidly admits that she has experienced enormous sadness, and even an unexplainable fear "In the safety of my own home. I would run up the stairs to my bedroom because I was scared, he [Schmitt] was behind me. I still don't go into banks if I don't absolutely have to. I do not feel comfortable. If it happens to you twice, I'm not going to push my luck."

At the time of the robbery-homicide, Sarah was engaged to be married. "I had already accepted a job in Baltimore, I just didn't get out [of the Bon Air Banking Center] fast enough. I never did go back."

Order

Sarah Orr said that Shelton Dunning's *You Need Order* life lesson has become part of her existence. Sarah said "I have no doubt that Shelton was our guardian angel on that teller line. Nobody else got hurt. There is no reason that he [Schmitt] shouldn't have shot every single one of us. He didn't; there was some higher power involved. I believe it was Shelton's doing."

Sarah Orr thinks about Shelton often. "When I'm going through tough times, I think of his advice regarding the power of orderliness. I tell that messy kitchen story. It made a huge impact on me for the last twenty (20) years."

"Whenever you go through a traumatic experience, you need order. It is going to help you heal, and help you feel better. This is what I could do for you!"

Shelton Dunning

CHAPTER 3

Southside Strangler

METRO RICHMOND, VA, 1987, Jon Burkett and
Steve Neal remember the cases well.

Serial Killer Terrorizing the City

Murder of Debbie Dudley Davis

A resident of Westover Hills observed something quite unusual in his neighborhood on the morning of September 19, 1987. A vehicle was found running but unoccupied. When quizzical neighbors investigated, they found that the keys were in the ignition, but nothing appeared to be obviously amiss.

Soon the Richmond Police Department was on scene. As is normal protocol, the officer queried communications and ran the license plate of the idling car. Registration for the vehicle came back to a residence that was one street over and a few blocks down.

The officer responded to the registrant's apartment, which was on the ground floor of an old, large, brick apartment building. The police knocked on the door, but they received no response. The officer noticed that the kitchen window was open, and that a rocking chair (they later learned that the chair had been stolen from a nearby porch) was leaning against the wall.

A neighbor came outside and asked if she could be of assistance. This neighbor was friendly with the occupant of the apartment in question. The neighbor provided the police a key to the apartment, which they used to make entry.

 Law enforcement found a nightmarish crime scene. A female was lying face down in the bedroom. The victim was identified as Debbie Davis, the owner of the running vehicle, and resident of the address in question. Ms. Davis' head was hanging slightly over the side of her bed. She had on only a pair of cutoff jean shorts.

The arms of Ms. Davis, 35, were tied securely behind her back with what appeared to be bootlaces. A dark colored sock was tightly twisted around her neck. A vacuum cleaner attachment piece and the sock had been used in concert as a ratchet type device to strangle and torture her until death. The victim's eyes were dotted red from ruptured blood vessels. For those who may not know, ruptured blood vessels in the eyes are telltale signs of strangulation.

It was evident to police that the victim had been sexually assaulted. Forensic technicians collected seminal fluid and hairs found at the crime scene. Analysis of the evidentiary hairs recovered from the crime scene indicated that the hairs foreign to the victim were those of a black male.

Murder of Dr. Susan Hellams

On October 3, 1987, in the early morning hours, a man returned to his Woodland Heights neighborhood home following an out-of-the-country business trip. He was sickened to find his wife, Susan Hellams, 32, dead in their bedroom closet. Though unnoticed at the time by the returning husband, police discovered that a screen had been cut outside the bedroom window. The screen was found lying on the second story porch just below the window.

Dr. Hellams' body was found seminude, with her skirt pulled up. She had injuries to her face and body that were consistent with a significant physical struggle. Her hands were tied behind her back. Two belts had been used as a binding around her neck. Law enforcement collected evidence that included seminal fluid found on and near her body. The medical examiner found evidence of a shoe or boot print on her back. The Medical Examiner concluded that Susan Hellams had been tortured, and that her death was the result of ligature strangulation.

Murder of Diane Cho

On November 22, 1987, two parents living in a Chesterfield County apartment went to work early in the morning as was their normal routine. As the day progressed, they became concerned that they had not heard from their 15-year-old daughter. The parents asked their son to check on his sister. When the boy entered Diane Cho's room, he was traumatized by what he saw.

The teenage girl was dead, nude on her bed. Her arms were bound, and she had duct tape across her mouth. Rope was found around her neck. Her feet and neck were hogtied together. The ropes had been used in a ratcheting manner to facilitate torture. Seminal fluid was evident on her body, and on the bedding. Hair foreign to the victim was recovered at the scene. Analysis of the evidentiary hairs from the crime scene indicated that the unknown hair collected was from a black male.

Diane Cho's Gavilan Court apartment was on the bottom floor. Her long rectangular bedroom window was but a few inches off of the ground. The bedroom window was found unlocked. The window screen was broken, and the screen was found lying on the ground just outside the window.

Similarity of the Three Cases

Virginia police strongly suspected that they had a serial killer roaming the streets. When Diane Cho was found, Chesterfield detectives immediately recognized that their case was likely related to those of Debbie Davis and Susan Hellams. The adjoining agencies met to evaluate known evidence. Soon, the two agencies joined with Federal law enforcement to form a joint task force. The singular job of this task force was to identify and arrest the vicious serial rapist and killer.

In comparing notes, the detectives realized that, at a minimum, all three cases had the following commonalities:

- Female victims
- All victims were found dead in the bedrooms of their homes
- All 3 cases occurred on the weekend
- Point of entry was bedroom window (screens broken and removed)
- Victims found nude or semi-nude
- All victims were bound
- The bindings were used in a ratcheting type manner to torture the victim
- Sexual motivation for the crimes was unmistakable
- Seminal fluid and unidentified hairs were found at scene
- Cause of death was ligature strangulation
- All victims had ties to the Cloverleaf Mall

How Timothy Spencer Became a Suspect

Murder of Susan Tucker in Arlington, Virginia

A 44-year-old female was found bound, raped, and murdered in her condominium in Arlington, Virginia on December 1, 1987. Local detectives investigating the case suspected that a well-known home-grown burglar (Timothy Wilson Spencer) may have been involved. As the detective investigated the whereabouts of Spencer during the Tucker homicide, he learned that Spencer had recently been paroled to live in a halfway house approximately 100 miles south of Arlington. The government transitionary home of Timothy Spencer was located in Richmond, Virginia, a straight shot down Interstate 95.

The Arlington detective then learned that Richmond detectives were investigating a series of homicides. When the Arlington Detective contacted Richmond Police, alarm bells started going off for everyone on the task force. Further investigation established that Spencer had traveled from Richmond to Arlington during Thanksgiving to visit his mother. The holiday was just days before Susan Tucker's body had been found in her home. Police also learned that Spencer's mother, Thelma, lived less than a mile from Tucker's home.

Task Force Focus on Timothy Spencer

Task force investigators quickly established that Spencer had indeed been staying at a halfway house for parolees on Porter Street in Richmond. Spencer had arrived on Porter Street 2-weeks before Debbie Davis was killed. The halfway house was a short distance from the Davis and Hellams' residences.

Police determined that all three Richmond region victims had ties to the Cloverleaf Mall. This mall was located on Midlothian Turnpike at the Richmond – Chesterfield jurisdictional line. Debbie Davis worked at a bookstore at this mall. Susan Hellams had made a recent purchase *from Debbie Davis* at the same bookstore. A jar of Vaseline found at Hellams' crime scene, was found to have been purchased at a store located across the street from the mall.

Diane Cho lived in the Chesterfield Village apartment complex, which is in very close proximity to the Cloverleaf Mall. Cho was known to frequent the mall with friends. Police confirmed that Spencer frequently rode a city bus to the Cloverleaf Mall. Spencer is believed to have stalked Cho when she left the mall and followed her to her apartment.

Police developed enough probable cause to compel a blood sample from Spencer. The genetic evidence was then sent to an independent laboratory for scrutiny. Analysis confirmed that Timothy Spencer had been at all three Richmond area crime scenes.

More details of the historical forensic connection to this case will be found in the *Story Behind the Story* segment that follows this report.

Arrest and Conviction of Timothy Spencer

Spencer was arrested and charged with killing the three metro Richmond victims. He was also charged with killing Susan Tucker in Arlington. Factual similarities

ultimately tied Spencer to the 1984 killing of Carol Hamm. He was never charged in that case, but the M.O. (modus operandi or method of operation) was so similar that detectives strongly suspected that Spencer was responsible.

Spencer was convicted of multiple counts of Capital Murder, Rape, Sodomy, and Burglary. Arrogant, defiant, and unrepentant to the bitter end, he was executed in the electric chair at the Greenville Correctional Center in Jarrett, Virginia on April 27, 1994.

Story Behind The Story

Proof Beyond A Reasonable Doubt

In solving the mystery of a criminal investigation, forensic science is often a game changer. In most sophisticated countries, *a confession alone,* is not sufficient evidence to establish the guilt of someone accused of a serious crime. In the United States, a legal principle known as Corpus Delecti, requires that proof (corroborating evidence), link a criminal suspect to the formation of a crime in order to obtain a criminal conviction. (Blair, 2015).

DNA has Changed the Law Enforcement World

Investigators have used forensic science to help solve crimes for centuries. Fingerprinting made categorical identification possible in the early 19th century. Photographic expertise modernized evidentiary data compilation in the late 1800's, and DNA (Deoxyribonucleic acid) technology absolutely revolutionized evidence collection in the late 20th century. DNA, the genetic material in the chromosomes of each cell, is frequently the evidence that links a unique suspect to a precise crime. The story that follows examines the ever-evolving impact of DNA technology upon criminal investigations.

DNA First Used in Criminal Cases

The first criminal court case that involved DNA technology occurred in 1986 in Great Britain (Baker, 2019). A young man stood accused of rape and murder. The government asked a biologist to utilize emerging DNA techniques to verify the confession of the 17-year-old suspect. DNA testing actually proved that the teenager <u>was not</u> the guilty party. A different suspect was later tested and confirmed thru blood analysis as the true offender. (Baker, 2019).

The first conviction in the United States that was based upon DNA occurred in Florida in 1987 (Cormier, 2005). In our case, Timothy Spencer was arrested in January, 1988. DNA evidence and the *Southside Strangler* made history when Spencer became the **first** criminal suspect in America who was arrested, convicted, and ***executed*** primarily on the basis of DNA evidence.

The Spencer case was also the very first time that DNA evidence was used in the U.S. to definitively link a suspect to the injured party. You will recall that semen and hair samples foreign to the victims were found at each crime scene in the Spencer story. Police evidence technicians meticulously collected and preserved the biological evidence. Private forensic lab, *Lifecodes Corporation*, was tasked with analyzing the physical evidence collected and comparing it to the sample taken from Spencer. It matched! The statistical likelihood that the DNA found at the Strangler crime scenes came from someone other than Spencer was one in 705,000,000 (Murray, 1992).

One of the First DNA Exonerations

Our *Southside Strangler* case also led to one of the first DNA exonerations in the United States. An Arlington County, Virginia conviction from 1984 was overturned as a direct result of the Strangler case. David Vasquez had "confessed" to the Carol Hamm murder that involved sexual assault and hanging. Vasquez was convicted in that case, and sentenced to 35-years in prison.

The arrest of Arlington native Timothy Spencer in 1988, made Arlington Detectives seriously wonder about Vasquez's guilt. They knew that Vasquez had a learning disability, and even though he had "confessed" to the crime, investigators were uneasy with eyewitness testimony that had placed Vasquez near the scene. There was also uncertainty regarding hair evidence. The prosecution had argued at trial that hair found at the 1984 crime scene was "consistent" with David Vasquez's hair.

The Modus Operandi for the murder that Vasquez was convicted of was a very close match to the Spencer cases. A private group of lawyers from the *"Innocence Project"* got involved in reviewing the Vasquez case. Following a thorough evaluation of the evidence, prosecutors, defense attorneys, and law enforcement agreed that David Vasquez should be released. Vasquez was pardoned by the Governor of Virginia. He was set free in 1989, after serving more than 4-years in prison.

The aforementioned *Innocence Project* works to exonerate prisoners who have been wrongly convicted of violent felonies. According to information from their website, there have been 367 DNA exonerees in the United States as of August, 2019 (Innocence Project, 2008).

Creation of DNA Databanks

In the late 1980's, several U.S. states began to create DNA databases of sex offenders. A high recidivism rate caused pioneers to focus on sexual offenders first. It didn't take long for the experts to realize the value of DNA across the criminal spectrum. According to historical information provided on the FBI website, by 1990, most of the early databases were expanding, including samples from all persons convicted of violent felonies.

CODIS

Criminals aren't bound by jurisdictional borders and boundaries. The Federal government recognized that a nationwide DNA databank would aid in the search for justice. CODIS (Combined DNA Index System) began in 1990, when the Federal Bureau of Investigation created a pilot program to oversee fourteen state and local laboratories (FBI.gov, 2020). The DNA Identification Act of 1994 directed the FBI to establish a National DNA Index System (NDIS) for law enforcement purposes. Currently, there are nearly 200 law enforcement laboratories across the U.S who participate in NDIS. Approximately 100 International law enforcement laboratories in over 50 countries use the CODIS software for their own database programs (FBI.gov, 2020).

How Does CODIS Work

CODIS uses a combination of science and computer technology to link violent crimes (FBI.gov, 2020). Federal, state, and local forensic laboratories are able to exchange and compare DNA profiles electronically. In a typical situation, law enforcement collects evidence from a victim. A DNA profile of the suspected perpetrator is developed from the evidence submitted. The "unknown profile" attributed to the suspected perpetrator is searched against the database of convicted offender and arrestee profiles (FBI.gov, 2020). If there is a match in the Convicted Offender or Arrestee Index, the lab will confirm the match and obtain the identity of the suspected perpetrator. Suspect information is then provided to the appropriate law enforcement agency for additional investigation.

CODIS Cold Hits

The expansion of DNA databases has led to a growing number of "cold hit" cases. In these situations, investigators have obtained DNA evidence from a crime scene, but they have no known suspect. Law enforcement submits the evidence to the federal DNA database. The query that follows establishes whether or not the evidentiary sample matches a sample from a previously convicted offender. If a match is found, a previously unknown suspect is identified and placed at the scene of the crime. In 2002, Virginia became the first state to execute a criminal convicted of murder and rape based on a "cold-hit." (FBI.gov 2020).

CODIS Metrics

The National DNA Index (NDIS) contains over 14,240,876 offender profiles, 3,998,467 arrestee profiles, and 1,026,054 forensic profiles as of May, 2020. (FBI.gov 2020). In addition to the raw data, CODIS tracks what they call "Investigations aided." This metric describes the number of criminal investigations where CODIS has added value to the investigative process. As of May 2020, CODIS has produced over 514,982 hits that have substantially assisted in more than 503,968 investigations. (FBI.gov 2020).

Future

The number of stored DNA profiles continues to upsurge dramatically. Due to massive numerical data, software improvements are among the highest priority for future planners. Familia DNA is an emerging area of focus in this field. Ancestral searching is a technique whereby a crime scene profile is run through various ancestry databanks in the hopes of getting a list of profiles that are genetically similar to the DNA evidence.

Investigators then use the information obtained to identify family members of the near matches. Due to controversy involving privacy rights and legal challenges, Familia DNA in the United States is currently used primarily (but not exclusively) to assist with missing persons searches, and cold case identifications. There is little doubt that the use of Familia DNA in criminal investigations will magnify as privacy issues are addressed.

Forthcoming DNA developments are limited only by the imagination. DNA phenotyping is a process of predicting physical appearance and ancestry from unidentified DNA evidence. According to the magazine *DNA Forensics,* scientists have already developed models that can accurately predict eye and hair color over 80% of the time. Soon researchers will be able to ascertain complicated facial features. In times to come, investigators will likely use DNA phenotyping to complete a depiction of their offender in much the same way that composite sketches have been used in the past.

CHAPTER 4

D.C. Sniper

RICHMOND, VA, 2002, *Jon Burkett and Steve Neal*
remember the case well.

Three Tense Weeks in October

Oct. 2, 2002, James Martin, a 55-year-old man was shot while walking in the parking lot of a Shoppers Food Warehouse grocery store in southern Maryland. Local police were investigating, but they had absolutely no idea why Mr. Martin was killed.

Oct. 3, 2002, James L. Buchanan, a 39-year-old landscaper was shot while mowing a lawn at a commercial establishment near Rockville, Maryland. Premkumar Walekar, 54, a part-time cab driver, was killed while pumping gas into his taxi at a gas station in Montgomery County, Maryland. Sarah Ramos, 34, was killed at a post office in Silver Spring, Maryland on the same day. A witness reported seeing a *white van or white box truck* speed from the post office parking lot immediately after the shooting.

Also, on **Oct. 3rd,** Lori Ann Lewis-Rivera, 25, is shot dead at a Shell gas station in Kensington, Maryland where she was vacuuming her van. And in Washington, D.C on this same date, Pascal Charlot, 72, was shot in the chest as he walked along Georgia Avenue. All six victims were shot with a high-powered weapon, and all of the homicides seemed to be random killings.

Law enforcement in Maryland and the District of Columbia recognized that they had a serial sniper working in their jurisdictions. Federal resources from the ATF (Alcohol Tobacco & Firearms), FBI (Federal Bureau of Investigation), U.S. Secret Service, and DOT (Department of Transportation), joined local law enforcement to form a task force to combat the evil terrorists in their midst.

 Charles Moose, the Chief of the Montgomery County Maryland Police Department, was appointed to head the task force investigation. Nationwide media coverage was incredibly intense, escalating by the minute. Hotlines were established. What followed was a strenuous, yet error filled investigation.

The sniper task force received a report following one of the D.C. murders that a blue Chevrolet had been seen in the area of that homicide. Chief Moose was holding daily news briefings. However, information about a blue Chevrolet was not provided to law enforcement agencies up and down the east coast.

Sniper Killings Continue along the I-95 Corridor

Oct. 4th, 43-year-old Caroline Seawell was wounded in the chest in the parking lot of a Michaels store in Spotsylvania, Virginia.

Oct. 7th, a 13-year-old student was shot as he arrived for middle school in Prince Georges, Maryland. Chief Moose and school officials reassured the public that they were tightening security and canceling all outdoor activities.

Oct. 9th, Dean Harold Meyers, 53, was shot and killed while pumping gas in Prince William County, Virginia.

Oct. 11th, Kenneth Bridges, 53, was shot and killed while pumping gas near Fredericksburg, Virginia.

Oct. 14th Linda Franklin, 47, was shot and killed in a covered parking lot at a Home Depot in Fairfax County, Virginia.

Northern Virginia police promptly joined the D.C. Sniper task force. As mentioned earlier, east coast police had been given a BOL (be on the lookout) for a white panel truck and later a white van as possible suspect vehicles. During the course of the investigation, thousands of white trucks and vans were examined by police via computerized license checks and traffic stops.

Law enforcement soon created and implemented strategic response plans that focused upon the Interstate 95 corridor. One such strategy involved stopping all traffic on I-95 immediately following the report of a long-gun shooting. As you can imagine, this undertaking was massive! The closed Interstate highway became a parking lot on several occasions as police searched for suspects.

Precious time and resources were wasted chasing the erroneous lead that the suspects were using a white van or white box truck. Law enforcement had contact with the actual suspects several times in the blue Chevrolet during the crime spree. However, due to the focus upon a white van, the killers were never comprehensively scrutinized.

Sniper Comes to Metro Richmond

Oct. 18th, William V. Sullivan, a priest at St. Ann's Catholic Church in Ashland, Virginia, received a telephone call. Details surrounding this important phone call are catalogued in the "Story Behind the Story" segment that follows this crime case.

Oct. 19th, Jeffrey Hopper, a 37-year-old male was shot in a parking lot of a Ponderosa Steakhouse in Ashland, Virginia. Ballistic testing connected the Richmond region shooting to the D.C. Sniper. Ashland Police, Hanover Sheriff, Richmond,

```
(oucono,un)
Ponderosa Buffet tel # _____
6:00 am Sunday Morning
You have until 9:00 a.m.
Monday morning to complete
transaction.
"Try to catch us withdrawing
at least you will have less
body bags.
              (BuT)
(ii) If trying to catch us now,
more important then prepare
you body bags.
   If we give you our word
that is what takes place
"Word is Bond"

P.S. your children are not
safe anywhere at any time.
```

Henrico, and Chesterfield Police brass were now also part of a sniper task force. A four-page letter from the shooter was found in the woods at the Ponderosa. The note demanded $10 million dollars if police wanted to stop the killings. The letter also contained a passage that said, ""Your children are not safe, anywhere, at any time."

In the woods behind the Ponderosa, police found a shell casing, a candy wrapper, and a plastic sandwich bag. These items, decorated with Halloween characters, were attached at eye level to a tree with a thumbtack. Post arrest forensic examination would reveal that the candy wrappers contained the DNA of both Sniper suspects.

The D.C. sniper case was now in our backyard. Locally, police were saturating all area's near Interstate 95. High alert, and constant vigilance were the order of the day. Every second of every law enforcement shift, fear and angst for our loved ones was real.

Suspect Citing in Richmond, Virginia

Following the shooting at the Ponderosa steakhouse, local and Federal investigators had reason to believe that the sniper suspects were likely still in the metro Richmond area. Investigators knew that the suspects had previously communicated with the D.C. taskforce via pay phones. Local police from multiple jurisdictions placed prominent pay phone locations under surveillance. A tactical decision was made to disable many pay phones in the area. Law enforcement hoped that the inoperable phones would force the suspects to find a working phone that police already had eyes on.

Oct. 21st, the sniper task force in D.C. metro traced a call from the suspected sniper to a pay phone at a gas station on Broad Street & Parham Road in suburban Henrico County, Virginia. The call for assistance from the Feds was mistakenly routed to the City of Richmond Police communications. Richmond Police sent the call to Henrico Police communications, and Henrico dispatched officers to the area. The first responding unit saw a white van pulled up to the pay phone at the Exxon gas station. The officer covertly observed this vehicle until the Henrico SWAT team could assemble and deploy.

News helicopters immediately responded to the area and filmed two men in the white van getting arrested. The vehicle was thoroughly searched. It was eventually determined that these men had no connection to the sniper case. Both were charged with immigration violations.

Through the investigation that followed, police learned that the traced phone call with the young sniper had actually been made from a pay phone at a Citco gas station. The Citco station is also at Broad Street & Parham Road; however, it was **directly across the street** from the Exxon. It is widely believed that Lee Boyd Malvo and John Muhammad actually watched the police take down the white van across the street at the Exxon station.

The fact that a white van (the publicly proclaimed suspect vehicle) happened to be at the Exxon station pay phone at the exact same time as the task force traced the call coming from a pay phone at the Citco station is an almost unbelievable coincidence. Failure to disclose to local police that a dark blue Chevrolet was actually the probable suspect vehicle, loomed large, and facilitated the escape of the snipers on this occasion.

Suspects Identified and Arrested

Oct. 22nd, Conrad Johnson, a 35-year-old male was shot and killed while standing on the steps of his bus in Maryland. The sniper suspects were now back in Maryland.

Though it hadn't been released publicly, police found a fingerprint at the middle school shooting on **Oct. 7**[th] that belonged to Lee Boyd Malvo. While investigating Malvo, the task force learned that he was in the company of John Muhammed. Muhammad drove a blue Chevrolet Caprice with a New Jersey license plate. Muhammad's ex-girlfriend lived near the capital beltway in D.C.

The sniper task force learned that Muhammad and Malvo had been traveling around the country for a few weeks. They began to discover that there had been at least seven deaths and seven wounding's involving "rifle" shootings in numerous states at the exact same time that Muhammad and Malvo were in those areas. Evidence ultimately linked the Snipers to additional crimes in Washington state, Arizona, Alabama, and Louisiana. Police compared Malvo's voice with the suspect voice messages that had been tauntingly left on the task force hotline. It was a match! Law enforcement was now confident that they had positively identified the D.C. sniper suspects.

The sniper task force decided that they needed the public's help to locate the suspects. Chief Moose announced to the world that John Allen Muhammad and

Lee Boyd Malvo were responsible for the carnage and terror. A description of the blue Chevrolet Caprice was provided that included the New Jersey license plate. Less than twenty-four hours later, a citizen spotted the suspect vehicle at a rest stop in Maryland. At 3:15 a.m., police converged upon the vehicle and found both suspects sleeping in the car. Overpowering force was used to get the pair into custody with very little resistance.

Law enforcement found that a hole had been cut at the rear of the 1990 Chevrolet Caprice for use as a shooting platform. The firing port, and a modified back seat, allowed Malvo to lie prone and remain hidden during the shootings. Police recovered a Bushmaster XM-15 rifle holographic weapon sight, a bipod, and a 20-round magazine.

Snipers Convicted and Sentenced

Lee Boyd Malvo, who was only 17-years-old during the crime spree, was convicted and sentenced to six consecutive life sentences without parole. Malvo's life was spared due to his young age. Malvo's attorneys continue his appeals to this day.

John Allen Muhammad, 41, was convicted in Virginia, and sentenced to die in 2003. He was put to death by the government on November 10, 2009 by lethal injection.

Story Behind The Story

Mayhem's Mouthpiece

"Initiate sniper task force" suddenly rang out across police radio transmissions! In minutes, both the north and southbound lanes of the main travel artery along the east coast were shut down in Central Virginia. On their way north, a Florida man by the name of Jeffrey Hopper and his wife stopped in to the Ponderosa Steakhouse in Ashland, Virginia. His steak, well done, but his departure to the parking lot was cold and bloody.

A single crack of gunfire. Without warning, a tiny place that calls itself the "Center of the Universe" unexpectedly had the attention of millions of people from all over the world. Instantaneously, law enforcement officers from all over the region converged on the small town of Ashland, Virginia, located in Hanover County.

Responding law enforcement agencies had been planning for the possibility of being thrust into the sniper pandemonium. Entrance and exit ramps were shut down on Interstate 95 and parallel alternate State Route 1-301. Traffic stood still. A sea of brake lights illuminated the night while police searched for the suspicious "white van" that had eluded authorities for weeks.

Media crews quickly arrived and made their presence known. A secure designated media area was set up near the Waffle House and Quality Inn on Route 54. The media staging area was about 100 yards across the street from where rescue crews worked to keep Hopper alert and alive. Hopper's abdomen had been ripped open by a single round fired from a high-powered rifle.

The regional task force commander appointed Lt. Doug Goodman as the incident's media liaison. He was in charge of corralling the cameras and releasing information about the shooting investigation. "It was the most amazing scene in my 27-years of law enforcement as far as media relations," Goodman recalls.

With the flip of a switch at two local CNN affiliates (WTVR and WRIC), the DC Snipers latest act of domestic terror was being broadcast all over the planet. "As the night progressed into the wee hours, cabs were showing up with journalists popping out. The Japanese media crew was the most, you know, wow," Goodman said. "That's when it really set in that this was getting big."

Lt. Goodman, who now serves as the Ashland Chief of Police, recalled the help he received from his counterparts in the metro area. "We had our local media partners showing up first and pretty quickly. I was getting a lot of help from Corinne Geller with the Virginia State Police, and Tom Shumate who was the Public Information Officer (PIO) with Henrico at the time. Without those two, I couldn't have done the job," Goodman said.

Goodman also credits his wife for helping to calm his nerves as he stepped up to a cluster of mics from all over the world. "There was a point around 2 a.m. when helicopters were hovering over the joint information center (JIC). I felt myself trying to overpower the rotor wash with my voice. My wife called and told me to stop yelling at those people [reporters] and to slow down."

In the early going, "It was easy to stick to the script and send out updates," Goodman recalled. In the beginning, authorities appeared at the microphones at the top and bottom of every hour. However, by midday, October 20th, police were running out of fresh news to release. Goodman said that law enforcement didn't want the message of "We don't know" or "That's part of an ongoing investigation" to weigh heavy on viewers. The decision was made to scale back the on-camera press conferences and let investigators focus on gathering clues.

Goodman had a special way of wrangling the media to keep them happy and interested. One tactic employed by Goodman involved feeding the media. Nourishing the media involved not only their stomachs, but their deadlines too. "We were on the northside of Route 54. Command approved me to take a convoy of cameramen across the street after we shut it down to get about two or three minutes of video. For the most part, that was sufficient and made those folks happy," said Goodman.

A box truck with Krispy Kreme donuts weaved its way through barriers. Goodman used his skills as a PIO to finagle box after box of donuts to give to media members working the story. At lunch, a pizza delivery would follow. Feeding the beast, (the media in this case) would prove beneficial to law enforcement in more ways than one.

The hours and days that would follow the Ponderosa Steakhouse shooting were filled with anguish. The snipers had shown that age was nothing but a number. Parents were doing whatever they could imagine to keep their children from becoming the next victim. "Our community was so supportive. I can remember at a local elementary school where parents lined the sidewalk to serve as a human shield for their children," Goodman recalled.

Following coverage of the arrest of the snipers, a woman told police that she had seen two men acting weird at a local Food Lion in nearby Tuckernuck plaza. She stated that a teenager had approached her in an aisle and asked where he could find Molasses cookies. It just so happened that they were right in front of them. She said, "Young man, they are right there." The woman said the disheveled teen then looked at her and said, "Have you heard of the snipers; I hear they are here." The woman says she felt like the young man was trying to tell her something, but she shrugged it off. Following their arrest, the woman said "Without a doubt," Lee Boyd Malvo was the teen who asked her about the cookies.

Divine Intervention

The Snipers bloody trail was littered with innocent victims. A way of life changed with every shooting victim that dropped. Pumping gas was at your own risk as it seemed the DC Snipers could be nearby. God willing, you were not in the crosshairs. What would it take to find out who the phantom shooter(s) were? As the number of victims mounted, surely, a mistake would be made, leading law enforcement to discover the identities of those who were evoking crippling domestic terrorism. While many in Central Virginia would be praying for the victims of such senseless crimes, it was another form of divine intervention that got the ball rolling in the right direction to capture John Allen Muhammed and Lee Boyd Malvo.

Monsignor William V. Sullivan, leader of Saint Ann's Catholic Church in Ashland, would pick up the phone at his Parrish a few days prior to Jeffrey Hopper being shot in the stomach outside the Ponderosa Steakhouse. The restaurant was about two miles from the front door of Sullivan's church. A disturbing voice on the other end of the phone asked about the "sniper shootings" and urged the police to look into a shooting that happened at a Montgomery, Alabama convenience store a few weeks prior.

This was not a confession, but an informational phone call. Monsignor Sullivan felt he had a duty to alert the FBI. "All he expressed to me was he had received this odd phone call and had been in touch with the FBI. Monsignor Sullivan instructed me, if asked, he would not be doing media interviews as his information was being used in an ongoing investigation," said Father Pat Apuzzo, the Catholic Diocese of Richmond's spokesman at the time. Father Apuzzo recalls it was a tremendously busy time for the diocese with the church already in turmoil due to the priest sex scandals. The DC Sniper call would only add more fuel to what was a roaring fire.

"[Monsignor] Sullivan originally thought the phone call was a prank" Father Apuzzo said. "When Billy [Monsignor Sullivan] called, he mentioned that he thought it was bogus because the caller sounded so crazy; he thought somebody was pulling his leg, I remember that." The caller had stated to the priest, "I am God," a phrase that would become a significant piece to the puzzle, connecting several crime scenes.

Investigators at the Ashland scene would find a note behind the steakhouse where it is believed the sniper crouched and waited to scope out his victim. The note specifically expressed that the author felt authorities hadn't been taking him seriously. The note, tacked to a tree, listed Monsignor Sullivan as someone who blew the sniper off. This clue triggered investigators in the sniper task force to meet with the Monsignor and ask him about the details of the phone call.

Father Apuzzo recalls that the note read: "They took my calls as a hoax or a joke and it has cost five more lives." The note also included the phrase, "For you Mr. Police...call me God!" The tip concerning an Alabama shooting led authorities to fingerprints that Malvo left behind at a crime scene in Montgomery.

Monsignor William V. Sullivan only spoke publicly of his role to police and in courtroom testimony. He died on New Year's Day in 2007. His sister, Peggy, has told newspaper writers that her brother never spoke of the incident and basically took the details with him to his grave. He was a man of the cloth, stuck in the middle of a violent mess that rocked the eastern part of the country.

Days after Monsignor Sullivan took the crazy phone call, the DC Snipers fury would end in a Maryland suburb north of Washington, D.C. Surprisingly to many, there was no white van; it was a dark blue, older model Chevy Capris. The triggerman in most of the sniper cases turned out to be Malvo, who would fasten his rifle to the carved-out keyhole of the trunk and squeeze off his deadly rounds. Cold and calculated, the teen would do as the older Sniper instructed.

Father Apuzzo mused that although it seemed that the duo may have run out of steam and were tiring from the killing spree, it makes one think, "What would've happened if the priest never mentioned the call and if the note was never left behind?" The circumstances of the capture does beg the question, did the Snipers seek divine intervention to save them from the clutches of evil?

CHAPTER 5

Tick-Tac-Toe

RICHMOND, VA, 1980, *Steve Neal and Jon Burkett know the case well.*

November 13, 1980

Social drug use in America exploded in the 1960's and 70's. Many young people in the Richmond region were engaging in their own poisonous mix of drugs, drinking, and illicit activity. Not surprisingly, countercultural pursuits often expedite volatile conditions that end in tragedy. The story that follows is one of the most brutal crimes in the history of Virginia.

Patricia D. Huber Cubbage, 22, from Roanoke, Virginia was trying to find her way in the world. Though she had a 5-year-old daughter, she found herself caught up in a lifestyle that was swirling out of control. According to court records and law enforcement sources, Ms. Cubbage was allegedly involved in prostitution, peddling drugs, and working as a police informant. She was living with, and socializing with, many like-minded risk takers.

The Night of her Demise

On the evening of her death, it was reported that Patricia Cubbage had been drinking and smoking marijuana with associates at her

Edward Fitzgerald, Sr.

apartment. Her apartment was actually a bedroom in a friend's home on Fallbrooke Drive in the Wynterbrook subdivision of Chesterfield County, Virginia. She had no idea that within just a few hours, the wicked recklessness of Daniel Johnson, and her former neighbor, Edward Fitzgerald, Sr., would end her life.

Fitzgerald and Johnson traveled to an apartment in Sandston, Virginia to confront an associate. Anticipating trouble, the pair took a machete to the confrontation. The pair had been drinking, and consuming pills. According to trial testimony, on the way back from Sandston, the pair consumed illegal drugs (allegedly "took a hit of acid"). Fitzgerald was said to be angrily proclaiming that Cubbage had ripped him off.

The pair decided to go back to Cubbages' temporary home and steal drugs from the residence. The drug and alcohol impaired duo forced entry into the home through the side door and pushed their way inside. Johnson testified that he searched for drugs while Fitzgerald went upstairs to the Cubbage bedroom.

Raped - Stabbed, and Cut at least 184 Times

Patricia Cubbage was attacked in her bedroom. She was raped and sodomized in her own bed while being terrorized with a machete. She suffered a cut over her left eye, and much loss of blood. Patricia Cubbage nearly lost one of her thumbs as she attempted to ward off blows from the machete.

Co-defendant Johnson, testified that Fitzgerald pressed the machete against his throat to hold him hostage. Johnson also testified that he was ordered to help Patricia Cubbage get dressed after the attack. Cubbage pleaded with the men, begging them to take her to a hospital. According to court records, Fitzgerald refused, and allegedly said that he had come there "To do a job, and that he was going to finish it."

Johnson and Fitzgerald used Johnson's vehicle to take the victim to a remote wooded area off of Newby's Bridge Road in Chesterfield County, Virginia. According to Johnson's testimony at trial, Fitzgerald again forced Patricia Cubbage to disrobe. Her clothes were left behind the automobile. Johnson said that Fitzgerald led her deeper into the woods, pushed her to her knees, struck her numerous times with the machete, and sodomized her yet again.

During the assault, Patricia Cubbage is said to have pleaded, "Please just blow my brains out and get it over with." The suspects continued to mutilate her by stabbing and slashing her repeatedly. When found, she had at least 184 (medical examiner said he stopped counting) cut and stab wounds from head to toe, front, sides, and back, including both eyes, as well as genital and rectal areas. A crude tick-tac-toe pattern was found carved in her back. Fitzgerald is said to have kicked her a few times, before he and Johnson covered her with leaves. Evidence showed that Patricia Cubbage died from loss of blood.

Aftermath of the Crime

Once in Johnson's car following the murder, Fitzgerald and Johnson consumed LSD in an attempt to forget what had happened. They drove to a remote area off of Newby's Bridge Road, where they threw Cubbages' purse out of the vehicle. When the pair returned to Fitzgerald's apartment at Jefferson Village, Johnson testified that

Fitzgerald told him that he was now "A one percenter." Fitzgerald allegedly tattooed "One percenter" on Johnson's arm and told him that he should be proud that he was an outlaw biker who had no respect for the law. Johnson showed his homemade tattoo to the jury at Fitzgerald's trial.

How Police Developed a Suspect

About 03:00 a.m., some of Patricia Cubbages' house mates returned home and found that she was missing. The blood and disarray in her bedroom led them to feel that something was horribly wrong. The victim's associates called 911.

While driving to the Cubbage residence in response to the report, a young Chesterfield County Police Officer demonstrated how important it is for police to be constantly aware of suspicious activity. Officer James Stanley observed a vehicle (that he knew to be Johnson's) emerging from a side street near a dumping area. He had often seen the car parked at night near Johnson's apartment.

Upon inquiring into the activities of Ms. Cubbage on the evening of November 13, the Officer learned that the missing Cubbage had been in the company of Daniel Johnson earlier in the evening. Returning to the isolated area where he had observed Johnson's car, Stanley searched until he found Cubbage's purse with its contents scattered nearby. On the same afternoon, November 14, Cubbages' body was discovered. Very shortly thereafter, Johnson and Fitzgerald were arrested and charged with capital murder.

City Man Charged In Bloody Slaying Of Ex-Neighbor

Richmond News Leader – November 15, 1980

Evidence at Trial

The prosecution introduced a large amount of physical evidence at trial. The supporting evidence included:

- Color photographs of Cubbages' bedroom
- Photographs of Johnson's automobile
- Photographs of the site where Cubbages' body was found
- Color photographs of Cubbages' mutilated body
- Cubbages' purse and its contents
- Cubbages' clothing and glasses
- A knife which was believed to be the murder weapon
- A primitive tattoo kit
- Pubic hair samples found in Cubbages' bed
- Bloody floor mats and a bloody newspaper from Johnson's car

Forensic evidence established that the blood found on the floor mats and newspaper in Johnson's car, on Fitzgerald's tennis shoes, and on a pair of blue jeans was that of the victim. Fitzgerald's knife was found hidden in his Lamar Drive apartment. The knife had Patricia Cubbages' blood on it. Pubic hairs consistent with Fitzgerald were found in Cubbages' bed. Fitzgerald's makeshift tattoo kit was also located in his apartment.

As he awaited trial, an inmate incarcerated with the accused, testified that Fitzgerald had told him that he had done it because she "Snitched on him and snitched on a friend of his also."

Daniel Leroy Johnson.

Co-conspirator Daniel Leroy Johnson was charged with, and found guilty of, first-degree murder. Johnson was never charged with capital murder. He received a 40-year prison sentence. There is little doubt that Johnson received prosecutorial benefit from cooperating with police and testifying against Fitzgerald.

Edward B. Fitzgerald, Sr.

Edward Benton Fitzgerald, Sr. was an 11th grade dropout who sat on death row for eleven (11) years. He never claimed to be innocent, and at one point he even told his lawyers not to pursue any more court appeals. He granted a July 22, 1992 interview to the Richmond Times Dispatch where he pleaded with young people to "stay free of drugs." Fitzgerald was quoted saying that "he hoped that his fate would deter youths" from taking the same path that he chose.

Richmond Times-Dispatch July 22, 1992 - Photo – Clement Britt

Fitzgerald always maintained that he was drunk and high on drugs on the night of the murder. He never publicly wavered from his claim that he had no memory of the assault. He did not speak as he was led into the execution chamber, but he did flash the peace sign, extending two fingers on each hand. Fitzgerald was put to death on July 24, 1992, in Virginia's electric chair at the Greensville Correctional Center.

"The vileness of Fitzgerald's capital murder of Cubbage exceeded that of any of the cases which we have reviewed. The systematic torturing of his victim by slashing her with a machete and a knife, followed by comprehensive mutilation, reflected relentless, severe, and protracted physical abuse inflicted with brutality and ferocity of unparalleled atrociousness. We hold that the sentence of death is not excessive or disproportionate to sentences generally imposed by Virginia juries in crimes of a similar but less horrifying nature."

Supreme Court of Virginia 1982

Story Behind The Story

X's and O's

Tic, Tac, Toe is a game of observation and strategy. A game that millions if not billions have scribbled on a scratch sheet of paper at one point in time in their life. It's a game that was symbolic in the lives of brothers Edward and James Fitzgerald, but for two vastly different reasons. Tic, Tac, Toe is played with X's and O's. It takes three of each to win. Lt. Colonel James "Jimmy" Fitzgerald has no problem stacking up victories.

The First "O" – Oath to Serve Country

The first "O" that Jimmy would model his life around is the oath. Jim took an oath to protect his country when he enlisted in the Air Force during the Vietnam War. Serving with a security police force, the young man from the Bronx had a mental and physical toughness that led him to serve his country. "I volunteered to go in the Vietnam era and served in Thailand. It seemed a natural transition for me. My uncle Eddie served in World War II, and my uncle Jimmy was in the Korean War," said Fitzgerald.

During his tenure as an airman, Jimmy Fitzgerald would be in contact with his family at home. He recalls that he was really attached to Eddie, the baby of the family. "When I was overseas, I got more letters from Eddie than everyone else cumulatively. We were close, very close." It seemed that Jimmy's love for law and order was wearing off on Eddie, as he was working as a security guard at St. Luke's hospital. "He, at one point said he wanted to follow in my footsteps."

The Second "O" – Law Enforcement "Operations"

Jimmy took the oath again as he started a career with the Henrico County Police Department in the suburbs of Richmond, Virginia. It was a dream job, he wanted to follow in the footsteps of an uncle who had a storied career with NYPD. "I wanted to go into investigations because I really wanted to be like my uncle Eddie," Jimmy Fitzgerald exclaims. After starting in patrol, Fitzgerald would submit his name to command staff, hoping to be selected as a detective. "I think the Sergeant who was trying to ding me on my platoon as a bad ticket writer, actually helped my selection to become a detective in the narcotics unit," said Fitzgerald.

Rising through the ranks of HPD, Jimmy Fitzgerald would spend countless hours with his counterparts and command staff in the field. Boots on the ground, preventing and reacting to crimes being committed would lead to the second "O" - operations. Jimmy Fitzgerald, by every sense of the word was an operational all-star throughout his 40-year career in law enforcement.

Jim served as a leader for Henrico's Narcotics Unit for many, many years. Alongside his partner with the Virginia State Police, and in contact with law enforcement representatives from all over the Richmond region, Fitzgerald spearheaded a Drug Enforcement Administration (DEA) task force that focused on sniffing out big-time drug dealers dabbling in the cocaine, heroin and meth market.

"We had arranged to meet on the south side of Richmond for a kilo of meth. I really didn't know Eddie was involved until we started running phone numbers, but I really believe Eddie and whoever he was with were trying to pull off a robbery. Luckily, they never showed because Eddie had a propensity for violence and we had really done our homework. SWAT was in place, so, yes it was feasible if they showed I could've gotten into a shootout with my brother."

The Third "O" - Observant

An observant officer...our final "O." Jimmy's observation of a specific apartment on Richmond's south side would lead him to uncover that his younger brother Eddie was involved in the drug trade. "I can't put my finger on an exact time when Eddie went the other way, but I realized he was too far gone to right the wrongs." It wasn't the first bout with trouble that Eddie had during Jimmy's law enforcement career. In fact, the two, once close, had grown apart since Jimmy returned and joined the police force.

As Eddie took a life path that steered him away from the family values that his mom and dad had instilled in him, the more Jimmy began to emotionally detach himself from the baby of the family. "He started using drugs and dating this girl that I thought wasn't good. I'm not about to tell him who he can and cannot date, but I saw it going downhill." Jimmy says his youngest brother had taken on the identity of a "wannabe biker."

Jimmy and Harry (the middle brother) had a hard time identifying with that lifestyle, since they were city boys used to the urban areas of New York. The proverbial nail in the coffin for the Fitzgerald brother's relationship came when Richmond Police called Jimmy to come pick his youngest brother up from the police station on Ninth street. Jimmy, had been promoted to detective, 8-hours before getting that phone call.

Eddie had been involved in the malicious wounding of his wife Bonnie. "My brother had been working at the Exxon at the corner of Boulevard and Broad all day and at that time he was living with his wife Bonnie and another male friend on Marshall Street. He was tired and went to bed, but something woke him up and that's when he caught his wife and this guy having sex. I'm not sure where he got it from, but Eddie pulled out a .22 caliber pistol and shot his wife and paralyzed her."

The First "X" – Exemplary Career

Etch a line through all three O's, chalk one up for the win. Jimmy Fitzgerald would also have a run with the X's. The first "X" would be Jimmy's exemplary career in law enforcement. Representing the best of the badge, Jimmy Fitzgerald would work his way up the chain of command and end his career as second in command, Deputy Chief with Henrico County's Police Department. He never wavered from the oath he swore to uphold, although he was tested a few times by the troubled sibling.

When his brother Eddie was convicted of the heinous killing of Patricia Cubbage, Jimmy was asked by Eddie's attorney to step in and speak to the judge as a character witness. Before the attorney even finished the question, Jimmy Fitzgerald had already responded with a resounding, "No!"

The Second "X" - Example

The second "X" crossed off pertaining to Jimmy Fitzgerald would be example. Lt. Col. Fitzgerald always set the best example for those he led. He wouldn't put an officer into a situation that he wasn't willing to get into himself. His life is an example of someone who has integrity, not willing to bend for anyone or anything that would be detrimental to the oath of service he raised his right hand to decades before.

"Part of my legacy in law enforcement is between the book ends." Was there a signature moment in his career? "I think this was my signature moment when I didn't hesitate to say no to helping my brother. I was faced with, I either believe in what I'm doing or I don't. I've reflected on this and other things. I had 40-years on the job and I want it to matter. I want officers who just knew me as an assistant chief, to know that I did decades in the streets."

The Third "X" - Execution

The third and final "X" would be execution. Not only did he execute tasks during a workday in an admirable way, but the word (execution) has a literal meaning in his life. What are the odds you have two men from one family follow such different life paths? Jimmy's brother Eddie was executed by electric chair in 1992 for the vicious stabbing and sexual assault of Patricia Cubbage.

Did Jimmy Fitzgerald allow his brother's violent shortcomings to blemish his pristine career? The short answer is No! Does it have Jimmy, decades later, reflecting on that time in his life where his baby brother committed an unspeakable crime? Yes. In retirement, the incredible brother paradox is allowing the once hardened cop to soften up and speak to loved ones about a time in his life that could've easily caused a career to come unhinged.

Jimmy Fitzgerald is a master of Tic, Tac, Toe.

CHAPTER **6**

A Madman's Rampage

RICHMOND, VA, 2005, *Steve Neal and Jon Burkett remember the case well.*

Three Victims Assassinated in 15-Minutes

Tuesday, May 31st, 2005, was a typical, beautiful evening in Richmond, Virginia (RVA). Suddenly, a deranged man set into motion a killing spree that would unnerve the metropolitan area for more than twenty-four hours.

6:50 p.m., Richmond Police received a call about a shooting at the Hillside Court housing complex. When they arrived, they found 29-year-old Derrick Conner lying dead in the street. Witnesses said that Conner was walking down the street when a man pulled up in a vehicle. They said that the shooter exited the vehicle, walked up to Conner, and shot him dead with no provocation. The killer took money from other individuals at the shooting scene before fleeing in a blue automobile.

7:00 p.m., Just 10-minutes after the Conner murder, a man entered the James Food Mart in a small strip mall on Broad Rock Road. Surveillance video recovered from the store showed the shooter walked into the convenience store and immediately approached the clerk. Witnesses told police that the shooter yelled racist comments at 43-year-old Abdulrahman Alabaman, a native

71

of Yemen. The killer then pointed a handgun at the clerk and proceeded to shoot him without provocation. Cash was removed from the register at the store, but witnesses told police that theft appeared to be an afterthought for the gunman.

7:05 p.m., The killer left the James Mart and went next door to the Poly Cleaners. Witnesses at the cleaners told police that the suspect entered the business shouting racial slurs at the Korean-American owner, 39-year-old Jong Doh. The killer pointed a handgun at Doh and shot him to death with no provocation. The killer fled the scene in a blue automobile.

Richmond Police stated publicly that they were investigating the cases as hate crimes.

18 U.S. Code § 249. Hate Crime Act

Offenses involving actual or perceived race, color, religion, or national origin. —Whoever, whether or not acting under color of law, willfully causes bodily injury to any person or, through the use of fire, a firearm, a dangerous weapon, or an explosive or incendiary device, attempts to cause bodily injury to any person, because of the actual or perceived race, color, religion, or national origin of any person

Identifying the Killer

Law enforcement had a homicidal maniac at large, running amok in a major metropolitan area. In a 15-minute time span, the same man had killed three people independently, apparently without provocation. It appeared as though anybody in the vicinity was suddenly at risk of being assassinated for no reason. Who would the disturbed man come across next?

In addition to interviewing witnesses, Richmond police focused on recovering video from the two businesses that had been robbed. In a very short period of time, law enforcement had grainy video footage of the crime at the convenience store. The video confirmed the seeming randomness of the killing. Video footage also helped police ascertain the license plate number for the vehicle that had been used by the suspect to flee the scene.

After communications ran the license plate number, police had the name of the registered owner of the vehicle that the suspect was using. Police cross checked listed titleholder information with DMV driver's license files. The photograph of the registered owner matched the image of the murder suspect obtained from crime scene video. Police now knew they had to find 26-year-old Daniel A. Bowler, ASAP.

Find Him Before Anyone Else Dies

Police were urgently hunting for Bowler. Everyone understood that the immediacy and unpredictability of the crime spree put every person in the metropolitan area at risk. Investigators worked to gather "background" information regarding the suspect's known associates and family members. Places where the accused was known to frequent became a high priority. Richmond Police contacted the neighboring law enforcement jurisdiction to their south since the suspect's last known home address was in Chesterfield County.

We Will Protect Innocent Residents – Take Him Out if Necessary

After the Richmond Police Department requested assistance in the hunt for the killer, Chesterfield Police quickly created an operational plan to check a home on Woodfield Road near the Wilkerson Terrace neighborhood. It was subsequently learned that the suspect had not lived at this home for several years. The current residents were new to the area and had no idea who had lived in the home previously.

Utilizing all investigative tools and techniques, the frantic search for the killer intensified. Since innocent residents near the City/County line were being systematically eliminated for no known reason, the Chesterfield Watch Commander decided he should discuss operational options with the supervisors under his command in the event that they confronted the offender.

The Watch Commander met personally with each of the supervisors who were on-duty at the time. After relaying known information, the leaders discussed the law enforcement duty to safeguard employees and residents. The Watch Commander then issued a directive that emboldened officers to preventively protect the lives of innocent people in their jurisdiction. The suspect was to be neutralized if he failed to immediately submit or surrender.

The Watch Commander authorized his officers to "Take him out, *preemptively if necessary*" to fulfill the obligation of protection of innocent life. Though a directive authorizing a strike against a killer might be controversial to some observers, the Commander was confident that his order would be supportable both legally and ethically.

Supervisory authorization regarding the possibility of an aggressive attack against a suspect is not an every-day operating procedure in any law enforcement operation. However, circumstances in this case, particularly the **ongoing threat to life**, the **continuing dangerousness of the offender,** and the **randomness of the attacks** made this a unique situation. It was the responsibility of the supervisors to ensure that all officers clearly understood the intent of the directive. The supervisors and officers responded with full support for their leader's unconventional order.

Apprehension of Daniel Bowler

Local, State, and Federal officers conducted a massive manhunt for Bowler after the murders. Hours into their pursuit, authorities were able to learn Bowler's cellphone number. A judge authorized a search warrant that allowed the use of an electronic tracking device to locate Bowler's mobile phone. Law enforcement traced the 26-year-old Bowler to a motel on Laburnum Avenue in Henrico County near the Richmond International Airport. SWAT teams and crisis negotiators arrested Bowler without incident approximately 20-minutes after they made contact. More details of the apprehension can be found in our *Story Behind the Story* segment that follows this report.

Record and Sentencing

Daniel A. Bowler's criminal record included assault and battery, robbery, use of a firearm, obstruction of justice, and a felony hit-and-run charge. As a juvenile, he had served time for previously robbing Jong Doh's dry-cleaning business. Bowler was also found guilty of felony malicious wounding in the beating of a juvenile jail guard. During the trial, a judge lambasted Bowler's criminal record and behavior as atrocious.

Daniel Andrew Bowler was convicted of three (3) counts first degree homicide, robbery, and of using a firearm in the commission of a felony. He was sentenced to

life imprisonment. At the time of this writing, Bowler is Inmate # 1127305 at the Wallens Ridge State Prison.

Hate Crime Follow-Up

Richmond Police Chief Rodney Monroe, ultimately backed away from the suggestion that the shootings were racially motivated. "There's no doubt in my mind that he was deeply troubled by relationships," Monroe said.

Story Behind The Story

A Chondrichthyes Crimefighter

When you hear the word "Stingray," your mind may wander to the ocean. Stingrays can be massive creatures that weigh anywhere from 100 to 3600 pounds. They are in the Chondrichthyes class of underwater sea creatures, adorned with a long tail that's used as a defense mechanism to fend off predators.

Why the oceanography lesson in the middle of a murder story? As you are about to discover, an electronic version of the "Cousin of the shark" was used to wash the stain of a deadly threat to society with calculated quickness.

A murderous rampage in mere minutes left a trail of terror, broken hearts, and bloodshed that paralyzed a community. A widow weeping, piercing intermittent screeches, and inconsolable screams. Racial epithets hurled prior to the pulling of the trigger. The unexplainable violence left police wondering if Bowler's motive was as simple and sinister as unfiltered hate. Police officials in the nation's 53rd largest market had a public safety emergency on their hands.

Law enforcement prides itself upon their ability to defend their residents. "Serve and Protect" can be found within nearly all law enforcement mission statements. In this case, investigators knew they were up against the clock. An overwhelming desire to defend "our citizens," caused palpable tension amongst the guardians. Immediate ground search efforts had failed to locate the suspect. Command personnel were desperate to use every tool at their disposal. A strategic decision was made to employ one of their secret weapons.

Electronic Stingray

In the 1990's, military operations in Afghanistan and Iraq began using cellphone tower site simulators or "Cellphone signal catchers" in the military theatre. A site simulator, or IMSI (International Mobile Subscriber Identity) is an electronic device with accompanying software that has the ability to impersonate cellphone towers. The surveillance device can track cell phone locations, intercept live phone calls, read outgoing text messages, or scramble nearby cellphone signals.

The Harris Corporation, a Florida-based company, trademarked a law enforcement cell tower site simulator device in 2003. The Harris Corporation produced the sizeable majority of law enforcement surveillance apparatuses (known as StingRay or Triggerfish) in the early years. Though StingRay is a brand identifier, original cell site simulators used by Law enforcement were typically generically referred to as StingRay devices.

It is easy to see how a StingRay device offers enormous potential to law enforcement. Police use the device to locate dangerous fugitives as well as missing and/or suicidal persons. They are also commonly used against street criminals, drug dealers, and everyone from petty thieves to heinous killers. A StingRay tracker in the right hands is a treasured tool for the good guys.

Legal Considerations

Privacy advocates have, and continue to raise, confidentiality concerns involving the StingRay's ability to collect data from unsuspecting users. The fake cellphone site is able to secure, record, and access personal data from countless phones whose users just happen to be in the area being surveilled. Many believe that the government collection and storage of personal data without a warrant is a 4th amendment invasion of privacy.

The legality and scope of intrusion from StingRay type devices is still being debated within the American court system. Although hundreds of State and Federal agencies utilize the advanced surveillance technology, only a handful of states actually require a warrant for its use. Most organizations have restrictive policy regulations, but to date there is no federal law that standardizes the usage of cellphone tower site simulators.

The StingRay Operator

Rick Reid joined the Chesterfield County, Virginia Police Department in 1979. The Hopewell, Virginia native and Radford University graduate, was selected as one of 10 recruits from a pool of 400 applicants. After serving as a uniform officer for five-years, Rick was transferred to the Detective division assigned to work burglaries. Four-years later, he was promoted to Sergeant.

A few months into his tenure as a supervisor, Rick Reid had earned an enormous amount of respect. He was named as the lead Sergeant on his shift, and he was placed in charge of his department's special operations. At the time, he was responsible for hostage negotiations, canine, aviation, search and rescue, and marine patrol. Two-years later, Rick decided that he preferred an operational position over supervision. He voluntarily relinquished his stripes, and joined a newly formed larceny from auto task force where he served for approximately 2-years. He worked several more years as a fraud investigator.

One day, the experienced Detective was asked to join another officer on a prisoner extradition. The task affirmed that arresting bad guys and putting them in jail kept Rick motivated. He sought an assignment on the Fugitive Task Force. Rick and another Detective reduced a warrant backlog from 3000 to 200. The assignment felt right, Rick said that he realized that he was exactly where he belonged.

In the latter stages of his distinguished career, the 22-year veteran had made quite a name for himself as a "hunter" of bad guys. He was a sworn special officer with the Virginia State Police, and he was also sworn to work with the U.S. Marshal Service. He served literally thousands of outstanding felony warrants. Shortly after being sworn in as a Federal officer, Reid found himself at the Technical Services Unit in Springfield, Virginia. Federal agents were giving demonstrations of several advanced crime fighting tools.

Just a few days later, Rick's own department was in a desperate search for a dangerous criminal. Using the U. S. Marshal Service StingRay apparatus, they had the suspect off the street in a short time. Rick and his bosses were sold on the value of the electronic device. Rick's agency used asset forfeiture funds to purchase their own StingRay machine. Over the course of the next few years, Rick would travel all across the State assisting fellow law enforcement agencies with StingRay search requests.

Capture of the Deranged Killer

As they were searching for Daniel Bowler, the Richmond Police Department discovered Bowler's cellphone number. Rick Reid would get the (SOS) call. Once he was operational, Rick plugged the necessary information into his tracking device. He learned that Bowler's cellphone had recently pinged off of a cellphone tower in the east end of the city.

When completing a call, cellular phones typically utilize a phone tower near the phone's physical location. When a cellphone signal hits the repeater of a particular tower, date and time data are recorded. This data can be retrieved by the applicable service provider. Usage of the tower is known as "pinging" off of the particular location. The tangible location of the tower gives law enforcement a radius of the phone's whereabouts when it was used.

Bowler's cellphone was pinging off a tower in the vicinity of the International Airport. Rick Reid used the StingRay device to narrow the parameters of his search. Instead of a long tail to thwart oceanic predators, the needle on an electronic Stingray machine points the direction of where the suspect phone is located.

By expertly manipulating the calibrated arrow & audible alert system, the skilled operator further refined the pursuit. Rick's precision probing led him to a low budget motel. The directional indicator focused his attention upon a room at the rear of the motel. Rick said, "As I got around to the back, the signal was showing hot." Task Force officers on the ground forced entry into Bowler's room and took him into custody without incident.

Rick Reid, and the secret *Chondrichthyes* weapon, ended the threat to life in Richmond on that hot summer night. The city, once again, rested easy. Interesting that several law enforcement IMSI trackers have fish names. Is it a coincidence that police use them to fish for fugitives? We think not.

CHAPTER 7

The Skating Rink and The Shallow Grave

RICHMOND, VA, 1990, Jon Burkett and Steve Neal know the case well.

In 1979, a roller-skating rink in Chester, Virginia opened for business. According to their website, the skating center is a "Family operated business whose mission is to provide a clean and safe environment for the community to enjoy

the sport of roller skating. Over the years many thousands of children of all ages have enjoyed a healthy workout while skating to the beat of their favorite music in a family friendly atmosphere."

I'll Give You A Ride Home

On October 5, 1990, Charity Powers had been dropped off at the skating center by her mother. Charity's mother had plans to go out for the evening. The mother and a male friend had an agreement that the man would pick Charity up when the skating rink closed. Little did they know the innocent little blond-haired girl was about to be kidnapped, raped, and murdered.

Ten-year-old Charity was wearing a pair of blue jeans, a white blouse with black buttons, a jeans jacket, and white L.A. Gear high-topped tennis shoes. Following her evening of skating fun, the fifth-grade student at Harrowgate Elementary school waited patiently outside the skating center for the friend to pick her up. Charity waited and waited, but no-one known to her ever arrived. Charity's mother, Taryn Powers Potts, arrived home at approximately 03:00 a.m. the following morning, discovered that Charity was not home, and immediately called the police.

Investigation

Police responded to the report of the missing child. Early in the investigation, police were able to locate a witness who had seen Charity sitting outside the skating rink after closing hours. The witness told police that it was approximately 12:50 a.m. when he saw the young girl. Fearing for her safety, the witness asked Charity if he could give her a ride home. Charity declined, and said that she was waiting for a friend.

The male who was supposed to pick Charity up on the night of her disappearance, told police that he didn't pick her up because he had fallen asleep. He said that he was very tired from working. His story was undoubtedly possible, but the account seemed odd and implausible. Valuable investigative time was consumed as police tried to determine whether or not the self-described sleeper was involved with Charity's disappearance. Law enforcement understood that this man could not immediately be eliminated as a potential suspect.

News coverage of the missing ten-year-old girl was intense. Soon, police located a witness who told them that "Late at night" he had seen a crème-colored station wagon with wood grain siding, cruising a nearby fast-food restaurant parking lot in Chester, Virginia. He described a man with long hair and a ragged appearance standing next to a young female in front of a fast-food restaurant around 1:00 a.m. on the night of the disappearance. This restaurant is located only a few hundred yards from the skating rink.

Within days of the disappearance, police had begun focusing on Everette Lee Mueller, 42, as a potential suspect. Mueller lived in the area, he matched the physical description of the man seen talking to a young girl at the restaurant after midnight, and he drove a vehicle with wood grain panels on the sides. Background and record checks revealed that Mueller had a long criminal history that included multiple sexual assaults.

Interrogation

During Mueller's initial interview with police, he admitted speaking with a young female on the night of Oct. 5 at the fast-food restaurant near the skating rink. He denied any further involvement. At this point, police only knew for certain that a 10-year-old girl was missing. No body had been found, and although they strongly suspected foul play, police did not yet have enough evidence to establish that a crime had taken place, nor did they have probable cause for an arrest.

Though unable to lock Mueller up at that moment, law enforcement was convinced that they were investigating a homicide, and that Mueller was the offender. He was placed under twenty-four-hour surveillance. During the following weeks, detectives put unrelenting psychological pressure on Mueller. Detectives tried to befriend him, one investigator taking the role of trusted older brother, another taking the role of a father figure.

Confession

Law enforcement relentlessly tracked and interrogated Mueller for months. They made contact with him repeatedly. Finally, during one of his many videotaped station house interviews, Mueller stated that he knew where a young women's body was buried. Mueller said he came across a body while walking through the woods. He said that he was afraid that police would blame him for her death.

Police turned up the heat on Mueller. According to trial testimony, Mueller ultimately told investigators that he had been drinking heavily on the night of the murder. He said that he thought that Charity was much older, and that he had initially approached her with sexual intent. Mueller admitted that he raped the young girl. Mueller also said that he strangled Charity because he was afraid that she would report the incident to the police. Finally, Mueller stated that he had purchased a shovel, buried the body, and burned Charity's clothes and jewelry nearby.

At the conclusion of Mueller's confession, court records show that he said to investigators "Let me shake your hand. Both of you. Y'all are good detectives. Y'all got the right man."

Body Buried in a Shallow Grave

Following Mueller's admission, Police were searching a wooded area a few hundred yards from Mueller's home. Police recruits, the department's search team, and canines from both the Department of Corrections (DOC) and the State Police were on foot combing the grounds. As the cadaver dogs were signaling an alert, the search team leader happened to see a small clump of blond hair sticking up from the dirt under his feet. Police had found the body of Charity Powers. A clump of hair and some bone was all that was visible above the ground. The primitive burial site was in a wooded area off of Rock Hill Road, only 900 feet thru the woods from the Mueller residence.

Police forensic technicians planned to carefully exhume the body from the location. They knew that the cold ground would have remarkable preservation qualities for a human body that had been buried underground for four-months. The painstakingly slow and tedious excavation would take days to complete. Law enforcement officials guarded the gravesite around the clock. For several cold, dark nights in a row, police officers actually sat alone with the body at the shallow grave in the woods – babysitting if you will. This was done to protect the crime scene and establish evidentiary chain of custody. Safeguarding the integrity of the evidence ensured that any items recovered during the search could be used in court.

Evidence Found at or Near the Scene

When police recovered the body of Charity Powers, they found that she had substantial injuries. The medical examiner established that her throat had been cut, and that she had an acute neck injury. She had nicks in the bone at the back of the neck that were thought

to be indicative of a knife slice rather than stabbing. There were bluish ink stains imprinted on various parts of Charity's body along with an imprint of the letter "E" in the middle of her back.

Police searched the area near Mueller's home. Court records indicate that they found a bone sticking out of the ground and a knife believed to be the murder weapon, 174 feet away from his house. Buttons from Charity's jean jacket, zippers from the pocketbook, and an earring that her good friend had given her for a birthday present, were discovered in the woods. Remnants of the jacket, shirt, pants, shoes, and the purse were found burned nearby, just as Mueller had stated.

Sentencing and Execution

Everett Lee Mueller was convicted of Capital Murder, Rape, and Abduction. He was sentenced to death on Dec. 19, 1991. Four different women (including one who was a relative) testified that he had raped them at knife point. A clinical psychologist who examined Mueller, was asked by the prosecutor; "Seems as if he [Mueller] is just plain mean, is that a fair statement?" "I haven't seen anything to the contrary," was the reply of the psychologist. Court records show that in response to questions from a prosecutor at his sentencing hearing, Mueller angrily said, "You want to put me on death row, that's no goddamned problem," and "Get this shit over with so I can go smoke."

Mueller's wish was granted by the State of Virginia. He was executed by lethal injection on 9-16-1999 at the Greensville Correctional Center in Jarratt, Virginia.

Story Behind The Story

Cherry Lee

When twenty-five-year-old Taryn Powers Potts learned that she was pregnant with her first child, she was ecstatic. Excited anticipation made the dawning of a new decade the best of times for the expectant mother. On July 15, 1980, following a twenty-three-hour labor, a beautiful baby girl was placed in Taryn's loving arms. Momma was very happy and proud of Charity, the only granddaughter in the family at that time.

Taryn lovingly recalls her baby's bright blue eyes. "We couldn't believe how active she was; right away she was moving her head all around." Taryn said that she could tell that Charity was full of life, "Ready to take on the world." Momma Powers Potts said that Charity favored her, and that she (Taryn) had secretly hoped that her first born child would be a girl.

The Early Days

It didn't take long for the toddler to acquire a nickname that stuck. Taryn recalled that she took to calling the little girl Cherry Lee instead of Charity. To this day, Taryn has a soft spot for the sweet pet name of Cherry Lee when talking about her daughter.

One of Taryn's most vivid memories of Charity's early years involved her daughter's love of swimming. By the age of two, Cherry Lee "Would stay in a pool for as long as you would let her," said her mother. She took swimming lessons for several years at the YMCA. The family often enjoyed time together at the Pocahontas

State Park, where they would swim and share private time. Charity frequently told everyone within earshot that she "Wanted to be a lifeguard" when she got older.

Taryn Powers Potts also recalled that Cherry Lee named her first and favorite doll "Pettles." Like most young girls, Pettles spent a lot of time with Cherry Lee, and played a very important role in her early childhood development. At the age of three, Charity began attending the Wee Folk nursery school. Over the next couple of years, dancing, and dance lessons held a special place in her heart. "She loved to dance," said Taryn. Mom fondly remembers how proud she was to attend several dance recitals starring her little performer.

School Age Years

Those that have children can easily identify with Taryn's memories of her little girl's first day of school. Taryn recalls how she and Charity were both a bit nervous at the bus stop. Taryn said that she was "Used to taking Cherry Lee with me everywhere that I went. It felt odd when the bus took her away that first day. Naturally, I missed her" said Taryn. Pride, and the realization that Charity was transitioning into a new phase of life made "That first day very special."

The next few years highlighted multiple interests for the pleasant, smiling, independent child. Charity liked to color, and she demonstrated quite the creative flair. Rainbows were common in Cherry Lee's early drawings. Ms. Powers Potts was full of pride when Charity won praise for her remarkable illustration of the Statue of Liberty during the "Freedom" art contest at school.

Artistic talent showed itself once again when Charity entered a young author's contest in the fifth grade. Contestants were required to create, write, and illustrate a story for the project.

Pettles the Talking Flower won first place among all fifth-graders at her school. Cherry Lee's favorite doll, "Pettles" clearly provided noteworthy inspiration to the young artist.

Taryn Powers Potts fondly remembers sharing many good times with her friendly, cheerful little girl. Taryn advised that she served as a room mother, read to the children's class, and ate lunch with Cherry Lee at school. At this point in her life, Charity would often say that she wanted to be a teacher. Taryn remembers that her daughter would gather little kids together and teach lessons to *her students.*

Taryn relayed that she and her family always possessed a strong faith in God. Ms. Powers Potts stated that she took her children to church, and that Charity absolutely loved vacation bible school. Mom was particularly touched by a note she found in Charity's bedroom that she says described the essence of her baby girl. "No matter who you are or what you look like, I love you," Cherry Lee wrote.

Some of Charity's childhood friends have described her as a typical All-American girl. She loved to shop at the mall, and go roller skating. It has been said that Charity and her friends could talk on the phone for hours. They regularly listened to music on radio station Q-94, made fun of boys, and busied themselves with typical youthful schoolgirl pursuits.

Bad Vibes - Fateful Trip to the Skating Center

Ms. Powers Potts vividly recalls the car ride to the skating center on that infamous Friday night in 1990. While enroute, another vehicle struck Taryn Powers Pott's car in the rear. The striking vehicle was totaled, but neither Taryn, nor 10-year-old Charity were hurt in the accident. Police responded and worked the crash. Taryn said that she "Had bad vibes," and told Charity that they were going to return home. According to Taryn, Charity insisted on going to the skate center because she wanted to be with her friends. "Please let me go momma," was Cherry Lee's plea.

The on-scene policeman indicated to Taryn that it should be okay for Charity to go since she had not been hurt in the crash. In the end, Taryn relented, agreeing to continue to the skate center so that Charity could skate Friday night away with friends. Taryn stated that she stayed a while at the skating center before leaving for her engagement. With tears in her eyes, and her voice trembling, Taryn remorsefully said, "If I had did what I thought, I regret it, but I can't take it back."

She Never Came Home

When Taryn Powers Potts got home on the night of Charity's disappearance and found out that she wasn't there, "I was absolutely hysterical!" Taryn advises that she immediately went looking for Cherry Lee. She went to the skate center, the Hardees, the Pizza Hut, and to nearby gas stations. No-one indicated that they had seen the young girl.

"I knew that something was wrong," Taryn said. "I felt it; I was all to pieces." Ms. Powers Potts said that she thought "My life will never be the same again." As the sun came up, Taryn remembers seeing dark reddish pink clouds in the sky that looked to her as if they were crying tears. "God is crying," she thought. About a week after Charity's disappearance, Taryn says that while walking on her porch, she could literally "Feel God's arms around me. God was holding me up, [she said] God was helping me keep going."

Days Turn into Months

With Charity missing, Taryn and her extended family got to work. They created, printed, and distributed hundreds of flyers. In the days that followed, Taryn said that she was frantic and desperate.

"Numb," she said, "I just couldn't believe it." Stress and worry made Taryn exhausted. "I couldn't eat, who could eat in times like that," she said.

At this point in our conversation, Taryn relayed a story about Charity's love of animals. Taryn said that Cherry Lee and "Frisky," the family dog, had a particularly close relationship. Taryn said that when Charity went missing, the male Cocker Spaniel knew immediately that something was terribly wrong. Frisky "cried and cried" loudly for 4-5 days after Charity didn't come home. The "Poor family dog was never the same after Cherry Lee's disappearance," said Taryn.

As the days turned from weeks to months, Ms. Powers Potts gave a lot of media interviews. She instinctively knew that it was important to keep Charity's story in the news. She never gave up hope of finding Cherry Lee alive. Even when law enforcement arrived to tell her the dreaded news, Taryn says that it didn't seem real. "I just didn't want to believe it" she said.

My Heart was Ripped Right Out of My Body

Taryn Powers Potts and family have experienced unfathomable pain and loss. "I don't know if you can understand this," she said, but "My heart was ripped right out of my body. She was my joy and sunshine. She made my world a brighter place." Momma Powers Potts did not get to experience Cherry Lee growing up; dating, high school, college, her wedding, grandchildren. "I missed EVERYTHING," said Taryn.

Losing a child in such a cruel way isn't fair, and simply should not happen. Closing in on three decades after her disappearance and death, Potts still has a hard time dealing with the loss of her daughter. In spite of it all, Taryn Powers Potts said "I have a strong faith, I take comfort in knowing that I'll see her [Cherry Lee] again."

CHAPTER 8

Memorial Day Madness

Richmond, Va. 2019, Steve Neal and Jon Burkett know the case well.

May 26, Memorial Day, functions as the unofficial start to the summer in Central Virginia. Hot and sunny, the stage was set at a southside park with a car show, a DJ spinning hip hop tunes, a petting zoo, and an area for kids to shoot each other with water guns. Unfortunately, it would be numerous real guns that would steal the headlines and turn the celebration into a memorable one for all the wrong reasons.

Just before 7:30 p.m. on that Sunday evening, the park in the Swansboro neighborhood became the scene of every parent's worst nightmare. Unexpectedly, with no warning, a gun battle between rivals caused a hailstorm of bullets to rain down upon the gathered innocents. Caught in the backdrop of what sounded like a war zone, people scurried, scattered, and ran for cover.

When the shooting stopped, two young children lay motionless on the ground, suffering from life-threatening gunshot wounds. Parents hurried to the aid of their children, scooping them off the ground and rushing them to the hospital. Those gathered at the scene were in shock, utterly disbelieving what they had just experienced.

Crime Scene Investigation

Responding officers from the Richmond Police Department kicked into overdrive. Every officer that we have ever known has a special place in his or her heart for the protection of children. When a child is hurt, police emotions run high. Trust us when we say, the way that we feel, and the way that even the most seasoned professional responds, is just different when young children are involved.

There is something especially traumatic about the serious injury or death of an innocent child. We have seen grown men break down and cry like a baby upon completion of heroic acts on behalf of an innocent little person. Many first responders experience recurring nightmares following interaction with child victims. Images of absolute horror are vividly burned into our memory, so much so that we can never, ever, forget what we have experienced. Most will tell you that they would give anything to forget what they have seen.

Taking you back to our Carter/Jones park crime scene, law enforcement had an extremely difficult investigation. Several victims and witnesses had already left the scene. Those that remained were in shock. The crime scene was large and unrestrained. Retrieval of physical evidence was difficult. Since the shooters were some distance away when the shooting started, and uninvolved in park activities, there was very little suspect information.

Richmond Police detectives working the case believed that there was more than one shooter in the incident. Police also hoped that someone in attendance filming cellphone video moments prior to the shots ringing out, may have accidentally captured photographic evidence of the killers. A forensics team was examining an area around the skate ramps, as well as another section of the park. Officials knew that even the smallest detail could be helpful to investigators.

Victims

Richmond Police said at a press conference that an adult male victim had reported minor injuries from the shooting. An 11-year-old boy shot in this case was treated and ultimately released at a nearby hospital. The 9-year-old Chesterfield girl who was shot died at MCV hospital. She was identified by family members as Markiya Dickson.

Long-Term Investigation

Not long after the shooting, the Richmond Police Department released the following suspect information:

Suspect 1 - A young black male who was seen with no shirt on and wearing a white towel or T-shirt on his head. He is believed to have braids that were shoulder length

Suspect 2 - A young black male with a medium build and short cropped hair. He was seen wearing a blue shirt and grey or dark colored pants

Suspect 3 - A young black male wearing dark clothing

Police pleaded with the public, asking for anyone with information to come forward.

July 3 – The Federal Bureau of Investigation (FBI) and the Richmond Police Department held a news conference at Richmond Police headquarters. Jointly, they announced that

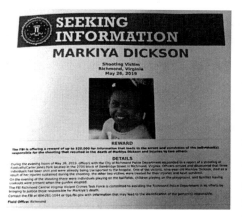

they were offering $20,000 reward to anyone providing information leading to an arrest and conviction in the case.

At the same press conference, a Richmond Police Lieutenant said that two groups had been fighting near the park. Detectives believed that there had been more than one gunman, and they believed that the shooting was not a random act. Police further said they had "Received a lot of information from the community about the case, but that they were still asking for an eyewitness to come forward to link all the pieces together."

Police Announce Arrests in Case

Nov. 1 – Police Announced that Jermaine Davis, 21, and Quinshawn Betts, 18, had been arrested in the Markiya Dickson homicide. The third suspect, Jesus Turner, 20, was arrested by the U.S. Marshals Regional Fugitive Task Force just before Christmas. All three men were charged with Murder, Malicious wounding, and Use of a firearm in the commission of a felony.

Richmond Police Chief William Smith stated that "These arrests can be attributed to two main factors. Great work by a team of detectives, and tips received from residents who were outraged by the death of a young child."

Jermaine Rokee Davis, Quinshawn Julius Betts, and Jesus Lamont Turner were each charged with: Murder in the 1st Degree,

Jermaine Davis Quinshawn Betts Jesus Turner

Use of Firearm in the Commission of a Crime, and Malicious Wounding.

Betts was found guilty of Second-degree murder, Malicious Wounding and two counts of Using a Firearm in Commission of a Felony. He was sentenced to 68 years in prison with 46 years suspended.

Jermaine Davis' was found guilty of Second-degree murder, using a firearm in commission of murder, Malicious wounding, and Using a firearm in commission of malicious wounding. The jury recommended Davis be sentenced to 33 years in prison. Davis will be formally sentenced on February 18, 2021. His lawyer said they intend to appeal.

Jesus Turner is scheduled to go on trial in 2021.

Story Behind The Story

JUST 5 MORE MINUTES

A day that was supposed to be full of fellowship and community fun for families in south Richmond, turned out to be a nightmare for Mark Whitfield and his wife Ciara Dickson. The day before Memorial Day, 2019, at the Carter Jones Park off of Bainbridge Street turned into the OK corral by a bunch of street thugs who thought they'd blow off some steam by spraying the community event with lead. Young and innocent children were caught in the crossfire.

An adult male and an 11-year- old boy would survive the gun shots after spending a few days recovering at Chippenham Hospital. However, May 26, 2019, Markiya Dickson would become a household name in Central Virginia for a very tragic reason. The 3rd grade girl, who loved Justin Bieber, was running to see a friend when a bullet hit her. She collapsed on scene.

Markiya Simone Dickson's mother said that she was a feisty, third grader who loved to dance. She had been practicing a Justin Bieber song to sing at her school's upcoming talent show. "We just wanted to take them out, to have fun with them," Markiya's father Mark Whitfield said. "We were just about to leave, and my daughter saw a friend."

"My baby [started running] and was trying to make it back to safety," Markiya's mother Ciara Dickson said. "I ran through the bullets and found my baby lying on the ground bleeding," Mark said. "That was my world, my everything." Mark Whitfield, would pick up his middle child's lifeless body and rush her to a

Mark Whitfield & Ciara Dickson

local hospital where she would later be pronounced dead. As he held his daughter in his arms, he said he could feel that a reckless gunman had ruined his life by taking his child from him long before her time.

Markiya's parents want everyone to know that their nine-year-old girl "loved everybody she met. My baby has a name," Mark said. "She was my everything, a part of my heart is missing," Ciara said. "Bullets have no name on them, people are so ignorant," her mother added. "I always knew my baby was going to be somebody special, said Mark. Now that's gone."

A Mom and Dad who left home with three children, but returned with only two, would give anything to have "Just 5-more minutes" with their little angel.

CHAPTER 9

"Smoke"

RICHMOND, VA 1992, *Steve Neal and Jon Burkett know the case well.*

Creepy Burglar

Authorities were facing an ominous challenge. During a regional meeting, crime analyst and Detectives discovered that homeowners in both Richmond and Chesterfield were experiencing numerous residential night-time burglaries in the same geographic area. While comparing notes, police in both jurisdictions realized that one offender was most likely responsible for a very large number of late-night break-ins to occupied houses.

The villain seemed to delight in making sure that his victims knew that he was in their home in the middle of the night. This suspect frequently stood at the foot of the victim's bed, staring at, or taunting the victim until they woke up. On several occasions the outlaw touched or spoke to the victims. Once the sleeping prey was mindful of the bad guy's presence, the thief fled the residence with items that he had stolen.

Law enforcement was concerned. They feared that this particular offender would escalate to violent sexual or homicidal behavior. The public was at risk, and the Police were feeling the pressure.

How Police Developed a Suspect

In the early 1990's, the Chesterfield County Police Department in Virginia had one of the most sophisticated crime analysis teams on the East Coast. As a unit, the all-female civilian squad possessed nearly 30-years of experience. They read every report, analyzed officer contacts, studied patterns, and dissected trends. They tracked and categorized arrests, prepared charts and graphs, and worked with other law enforcement resources to identify potential offenders.

Based upon their studies and collaboration, it didn't take long for regional analysts to identify Donald Coleman as a promising target. Coleman was a long-time, habitual criminal who lived in the area. He matched the general physical description provided by some of the victims, and his criminal rap sheet made it clear that he was a dangerous offender whose specialty was burglary, assault, and larceny. Crime fighters also knew that a close relative of Coleman was incarcerated for night-time burglary and rape.

The challenge for the good guys was that Coleman was a seasoned crook who was an expert at plying his trade. He always wore gloves so as not to leave fingerprints, and he was very careful to remove his burglary tools. He was known to use items from within the residence to carry his loot, and rarely, if ever, did he leave evidence behind.

One of Donald Coleman's many nicknames was SMOKE. One of the reasons that Coleman was known as smoke is because he had an uncanny ability to operate in stealth mode. He was so smooth that he had a reputation of someone nearly invisible. It seemed as though Coleman could disappear in an instant, as if he was able to go up in fumes.

Creating the Operational Plan

The Crime Analyst had plotted the burglaries from both bailiwicks on a map. The visual showed crime locations spread over several square miles. The neighborhoods were parallel to each other but separated by

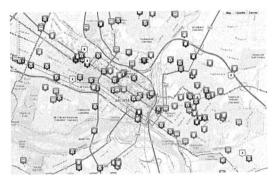

Crime mapping example, not from 1992

jurisdictional lines. It appeared as though the suspect may have been traversing the City-County line on foot. His victim homes to the left were in the County, victim homes to the right were in the City.

Detectives and supervisors met to brainstorm a solution to the unsettling burglar problem. Conventional investigative methods were not likely going to be enough to put the creepy burglar away. All understood that they needed to catch the offender in the act in order to make their case stick. Surveillance was the weapon of choice, but it wouldn't be easy to follow a proficient burglar on foot. It became abundantly clear that law enforcement needed to figure out how to give themselves an operational advantage.

Covert Investigation

Everyone on the covert investigative team took a preparatory field trip the following day. They walked more than a mile along the wooded area that was the jurisdictional line between the Richmond City and Chesterfield County cases. Even though the burglaries were occurring at night, it was important that they see the suspect's likely route thru the prism of daylight.

During the scout mission, it was apparent that a set of railroad tracks ran right thru the area between the two jurisdictions. The same railroad tracks were also a short distance from suspect Coleman's home. Detectives theorized that Coleman was walking the tracks at night, simply veering left or right to choose his victims. Following completion of the crime, the offender could unassumingly walk the tracks back home. It seemed likely that the railroad tracks were his navigational corridor.

Execution of the Plan

The operational plan was crafted based upon the discoveries discussed in the previous paragraphs. Detectives would position themselves strategically near the railroad tracks between Coleman's home and the potential victim neighborhoods.

You will recall that the crimes were occurring late at night while people were in bed asleep. The covert team decided to work an 8 p.m. – 4 a.m. shift. The wooded area along the railroad tracks was very dark at night. Detectives geared up, dressed appropriately, and prepared to spend some cold January nights in the great outdoors.

A handful of Detectives carried Night Scopes as they positioned themselves every few hundred yards along the railroad track passageway. The remaining Detectives were assigned to be mobile, serving as a response team able to react at a moment's notice. A K-9 tracking dog was assigned to work with the team as well.

The first night of surveillance was uneventful. The second night in the woods wasn't very exciting either until just before midnight. Suddenly, one of the covert Detectives heard a woman's blood curdling scream. From his position in the woods, the Detective could hear the shriek, but he had no idea which home (or even which street) was the site of the emergency. Some covert mobile response officers were immediately directed to two neighborhoods on the County side to investigate. The undercover officers were searching frantically, but they weren't immediately able to pinpoint a crime scene or a victim.

As expected, the next thing you heard were the alert tones from the Chesterfield police radio. They dispatched uniform officers to a home burglary in progress on Brentford Drive. The back yard at this location backed up to the woods and the railroad tracks. Covert officers and uniform police officers responded to investigate. An older female victim reported that she had been awakened by a noise. Upon investigation, she saw a small male, dressed in dark clothing and dark mask, standing in her garage. She stated that when she screamed, the suspect fled her home.

Apprehension

The covert officers on-foot in the woods were on high alert. They utilized Night Scopes as they scanned their area of responsibility. For those who may not know, a Night Scope is a small handheld electronic device that enhances the user's vision in the dark. Within 5-minutes of hearing the victim scream, the team's pre-planning and preparation started to bear fruit.

"I've got him sitting on the railroad tracks smoking a cigarette" suddenly came across the covert radio in whispered tones. One of the Detectives in the woods, Larry Covington, had spotted the suspect. At this point, the man on the tracks was approximately 200-yards from the victim's home, and approximately 1-mile from Donald Coleman's home. But there he was, sitting motionless next to the railroad tracks.

You will recall that our offender was a proficient bad guy. This suspect was smart enough to sit tight while overt law enforcement was combing the area. He was letting the activity "cool down," attempting to wait out the initial search by police. He hunkered down so as not to expose himself to discovery and apprehension.

The Detective relayed that the suspect was a short male dressed in all black clothing. The suspect had a black mask covering his head and face. He was wearing dark gloves, and he had a light-colored pillowcase by his side. Over the course of the next 10 to 15 minutes, the covert Detective continuously observed the suspect. Both he and the offender were sitting still, patiently waiting. The suspect finished his cigarette.

Slowly, the suspect began to cautiously move along the railroad tracks. The suspect was carrying a pillowcase over his shoulder like a knapsack. This suspect was walking in the direction of Donald Coleman's home. Other covert Detectives picked up the trail of the suspect as he walked along the railroad tracks. Due to effective positioning, the Detectives had him continuously under surveillance without exposing their locations.

The covert response team was quickly formulating its arrest plan. Supervision ensured that all train activity was halted along the tracks over the course of the next hour. The arrest team put

themselves approximately ½ mile northeast of where the suspect was originally observed. They walked until they found the perfect spot. It was so dark at this location, that you literally could not see a colleague standing more than three feet away. The apprehension team hunkered down in place alongside the tracks.

Patience, stillness, and stealth mode were paramount. The arrest team waited silently as the suspect slowly made his way toward their position. When the suspect came within 10-12 feet of the apprehension team, they pounced. The officers, with weapons drawn, vociferously lit up the scene and took the offender into custody.

The suspect was astonished, literally DUMBFOUNDED! His defeated body language was priceless. You could see the look of bewilderment on his face through his black ski mask. The bad guy could not believe that he had been caught red-handed. He was carrying the pillowcase of stolen goods in his hand.

Job Well Done

The victim of the home break-in identified the pillowcase and the items contained within it as property stolen from her garage. Donald "Smoke" Coleman was arrested and charged with statutory burglary and breaking and entering into a dwelling at night with the intent to commit larceny. He was also charged with the separate count of larceny. He refused to cooperate, made no statement, and immediately lawyered up. Eight-months later, a jury found Donald Coleman guilty and sentenced him to 5-years in the state penitentiary.

Law enforcement in both Richmond and Chesterfield were able to clear dozens of night-time burglaries in the area. Even though there wasn't enough evidence to actually charge him with more than one crime, the M.O. (modus operandi or method of operation) was so similar that that there was little doubt that he was the responsible offender. Coleman didn't admit wrongdoing, but police were certain that they had their man.

On May 20, 2020, Donald Coleman, inmate # 1063104 at the Virginia State Farm Correctional Center, was released from prison.

Story Behind the Story

Sanctuary Desecration

Home

Home is much more than a material place to reside. Most of us have a strong emotional bond with the domicile that we call home. A sense of who we are, is frequently intertwined with a passionate attachment to where we dwell. Adages such as "Home is where the heart is" and "My home is my castle" make it clear that the psychology of home is much more than fondness for a physical location.

When Dorothy from the *Wizard of Oz* was in trouble, she kept repeating the phrase "There's no place like home, there is no place like home." The mantra helped her to fight fear and torment. It is clear that during a time of great stress, Dorothy was seeking a place of emotional tranquility. Like Dorothy, we all treasure a space where we can feel safe, calm, and content on a very deep level.

What happens when human beings feel vulnerable in the very place where we need comfort and security? When a criminal enters your home without invitation, you will likely experience an overwhelming sense of violation. Immensely personal crimes inflict deep emotional damages. An invasion of the place where we replenish our energy, the place where we feel most ourselves, is a distinctive and consequential type of defilement.

The report that follows explores the devastation surrounding unlawful criminal encroachment upon a private residence.

The Right of the People to be Secure in Their House

Americans feel strongly about their right to be secure in their home. The Founding Fathers made property rights and home privacy a cornerstone of America's foundation. The Fourth Amendment of the U.S. Constitution enumerates "The right of the people to be secure in their persons, houses, papers, and effects, against unreasonable searches and seizures, shall not be violated. No warrants shall issue, but upon *probable cause*, supported by oath or affirmation, and particularly describing the place, person, or things to be searched."

Of the places protected from unreasonable search and seizure, a person's home holds a distinctly privileged status. Courts have bestowed an elevated amount of judicial sacredness to dwellings based on rights of confidentiality and privacy.

Breaking and Entering

Burglary is defined as the unlawful entry into a building for the purpose of committing a crime. Commonly referred to as a B & E (breaking and entering), burglary is the second most frequent crime in the United States. According to the Bureau of Justice Statistics (DOJ), in 2018, there were 1,333,600 burglaries in the U.S. where an offender attempted a theft. Mathematically, this equates to nearly 3 burglaries every minute, or roughly 3,654 unlawful entries every day.

Most U.S. States incorporate both the dwelling house of another, and illegal entry to a business in their criminal burglary statutes. Though often comingled, larceny is not necessarily an essential element of burglary. Most often, intent to commit "a crime" other than trespass must be present in order to classify the illegal entry as a burglary. Burglary into an occupied dwelling at night is typically considered a more serious offense.

Statistics indicate that the majority of home burglaries occur during the daytime hours when no-one is home. Many convicted burglars have told police that they prefer a vacant residence so that no confrontation will take place. However, according to Department of Justice (DOJ) Bureau of Statistic information, approximately 7% of all burglaries in the United States involve an innocent person who experiences violent victimization.

Barbara was Home when it Happened

Invading an occupied home and purposely confronting the victim unmistakably multiplies the level of menace. As you read the story that follows, imagine yourself being home alone when strangers force their way into your house! Even worse, envision the unknown intruder(s) awakening you from a deep slumber.

The story of Barbara is typical of thousands of home invasions that occur each year. Barbara (not her real name), did not wish to be formally identified for this story. Though this tale is technically not an exact transcript of her particular case (some facts and details have been slightly modified), the circumstances and emotions expressed in the following paragraphs are very real. Again, and again, your authors have heard the following home invasion details recited by many different victims.

Barbara is a typical 19-year-old college student still living at home. Her parents were at work. Mid-morning, she was dozing off, watching television, when she heard unexpected knocking at the front door. Peeping thru a bedroom curtain, she saw two strangers on the front porch. Seeing no car in the vicinity made Barbara suspicious. The two men eventually left the front porch. In short order, the men were at the rear of the house, now knocking at the back door. Barbara retrieved her cell phone and ran to the basement while calling her mother at work.

Suddenly, an enormously loud crashing sound sent terror shock-waves through Barbara's body. The criminals smashed the glass in the back door with a baseball bat. Shaken, and startled by the unknown, and then the realization that her life was in danger, created an OMG moment. Heart pounding, hands trembling, Barbara said that she was literally petrified and didn't know what to do! Her thoughts instantaneously ranged from should she hide, pretend to be asleep, try to reason with bad guys, look for a weapon, or physically fight with the intruders? Barbara's mother could hear the mayhem thru the phone, and told her daughter that she was calling 911.

Barbara momentarily thought, is this a dream, or is this real? Bewildered and confused, the sound of the burglars literally froze her with fear. The ransacking noises upstairs caused panic attack after panic attack. Somehow, Barbara was finally able to maneuver herself into the bathroom, were she hid behind the shower liner. After 4 or 5 minutes of plundering, the home got quiet. Barbara hoped that the burglars had finally left.

The next thing Barbara heard were the loud voices of men claiming to be law enforcement. "POLICE! POLICE OFFICER, they bellowed as they rumbled thru the house. Staring down the barrel of a gun, Barbara said "Please don't shoot me" when the officers found her hiding place.

The Aftermath of the Crime

Barbara, like many victims, told the police that the invaders took everything of value we had, and completely ransacked our home. She decided that it would be best if she stayed at a friend's house for a little while. Her family spent a small fortune buying security cameras and alarms. The Doctors put her on medications to help with her anxiety. Barbara tells friends that she doesn't even know how long it will be before she can sleep in her own bed.

What Should I Expect If My Home is Burglarized?

We hope that you never have to experience the anguish and sorrow associated with a home burglary. However, if it happens to you, you will likely be forced to confront many of the following emotions:

- Sense of personal violation
- Sense that home is no longer a safe place
- Shock and disbelief
- Sense of privacy vanquished
- Uncomfortable being alone
- Fear of another break-in
- Personal possessions rummaged thru and stolen
- Financial loss
- Anger toward the criminal
- Confusion and frustration with police and court system
- An urgency to protect home and property in the future
- Suspicion of strangers
- Fear of strangers
- Difficulty sleeping
- Eating disorders
- Anxiety
- Exaggerated startle reactions
- Stress of dealing with children who may have been victimized

Often you will hear burglary described as a victimless *property crime*. As you discovered in this chapter, nothing is further from the truth.

Chapter 10

Steak & Ale – and The Rosenbluths

RICHMOND, VA 1993, Jon Burkett and Steve Neal know the cases well.

Romance After Work at the Steak & Ale

Sheryl Lyn Stack and Edward Martin both worked at the Steak & Ale restaurant on Midlothian Turnpike near Chippenham Parkway. After working until closing time on Oct. 7, 1993, they decided to socialize at a nearby establishment. They traveled separately, Stack in her Volvo, and Martin in his red sports car.

A few minutes after 02:00 a.m. (last call), the pair drove back to their place of employment. An employee of an adjacent motel happened to be outside on a smoke break. This motel employee saw the two young people standing in the parking lot beside their cars talking and kissing. After a few minutes, the couple were seated in Stack's vehicle.

Shot in the Parking Lot

Trial testimony revealed that, suddenly, the smitten couple were startled by strangers. A man standing outside the vehicle held them at gunpoint as he ordered them out of the car. Martin testified that the armed robber told him to hand over his wallet and car keys to another man who was on scene. According to police reports, the mugger told Stack and Martin that if they would lie down on the parking lot and close their eyes, he would not hurt them. Both victims complied with the directions. Though he had promised not to harm the pair, the suspect shot them in the head as they were laying on the pavement.

Crime Scene Evidence

About 25-30 minutes after seeing Stack and Martin in the Steak & Ale parking lot, the aforementioned motel employee heard two loud "bang" noises. He testified that when he looked in the direction of the restaurant, he saw a car being driven from the area at a high rate of speed. This witness called 911.

A Richmond Police officer found Stack and Martin shot, lying face down in a pool of blood, with their hands touching. According to testimony at trial, they were trying to communicate with each other, but police couldn't make out what they were saying. Stack's car was ransacked, her purse and other personal property in disarray on the front seat. Two depleted .45 caliber cartridge casings, and two .45 caliber bullets were found at the scene.

Sheryl Stack died from her wounds. Edward Martin survived but suffered severe life altering injuries. Martin lost an eye, the use of one arm and leg, and he suffered severe brain damage. Though physically unable to communicate clearly, Martin bravely testified against his attackers when they were brought to trial.

Cocaine Addiction in the Suburbs

Family members who lived out of town had not spoken with Richard or Rebecca Rosenbluth for several days. Unable to make contact, the relative called Chesterfield Police. When police arrived, they found the home closed up tightly. No vehicles that belonged to the couple were in the driveway. Newspapers and mail appeared to be piling up. When the police were unable to make contact with the residents, the supervisor authorized forced entry into the home to check on their welfare.

Law enforcement found two bodies in the den of the home. Richard, 40, regional manager of a coffee business, had been shot twice in the head. His wife, Rebecca, 35, a secretary for a local sales distribution company, was shot 4 times in the head and neck at close range.

The Rosenbluth residence was not ransacked, and police found no obvious point of forced entry to the home. This evidence led police to theorize that the victims were most likely familiar with their killers. It appeared that the pair had voluntarily allowed the suspects into the house.

Evidence of drug use was obvious at the crime scene. Some personal items and the couple's vehicle were stolen. During the investigation, Chesterfield Police discovered bank records that showed that the deceased couple made substantial cash withdrawals and credit card charges (averaging hundreds of dollars per day) during the months immediately preceding their deaths. Early signs led investigators to believe that drug usage likely played a large role in these murders.

A .45 caliber gun had been used in the killing of the Rosenbluths. Police knew that a .45 caliber weapon was also used in the Steak & Ale robbery/murder. The two situations occurred just a few weeks apart, and only 4-miles away from each other. Victim vehicles were stolen in both violent crimes. Could the cases be related? Richmond and Chesterfield Police compared notes, looking for commonalities.

Suspects

Richmond Police recovered Edward Martin's car a few days after the crime at Steak & Ale. Although they forensically processed the recovered stolen auto, they were unable to obtain fingerprints or any other useful evidence.

Andre Graham, AKA "Panama" was incarcerated in the Chesterfield County jail on an unrelated charge. Graham made a telephone call in the presence of a Chesterfield County Deputy Sheriff. The Deputy reported this conversation to his supervisor. The Deputy testified that Graham told the person on the other end of his call, "Go into the closet, get the bag with the contents and get rid of it."

All phone calls in or out of the Chesterfield County jail are recorded. Police were able to determine that Andre Graham had been talking to his live-in girlfriend, Priscilla Booker. Detectives with the Chesterfield County Police Department went to Graham's apartment where they found the girlfriend. She gave a veteran homicide Detective verbal consent to search the apartment. The Detective found a .45 caliber pistol in a plastic bag in a linen closet.

Girlfriend Gives it Up

Under intense questioning, Priscilla Booker told police that Graham was close friends with Mark Shepard and a third man. She stated that on the morning of the Steak & Ale killing, she had seen Graham driving a car that matched the vehicle belonging to Edward Martin. She further advised that she and Graham had watched a news report of the Stack murder. She indicated that Graham made the statement, "He [Graham] knew who did it, but he [Graham] didn't."

Priscilla Booker told police that a few days after Sheryl Stack's murder, she found a box of over 200 compact disks in the trunk of her car. The girlfriend told police that Andre Graham said that he bought the CDs for ten dollars ($10). Booker told police that she put the CDs in a rented storage bin. Law enforcement went to the storage shed with a search warrant and recovered a large number of the compact disks stolen from Edward Martin's vehicle during the robbery/murder at Steak & Ale. A fingerprint expert later testified that 31 of the 48 identifiable fingerprints found on the CDs belonged to Andre Graham.

Cooperating to the fullest extent, Booker also told police that Andre Graham kept the .45 caliber handgun in his possession. She stated that she had been present for the transaction in which Graham had obtained the weapon. At trial, a firearms identification expert testified that Graham's gun <u>was the weapon</u> from which the cartridge cases found at both murder scenes had been fired and ejected.

Arrests

Chesterfield Police issued a nationwide BOL (Be on the lookout) for the 1988 Nissan Pathfinder that had been stolen from the Rosenbluth home. Police in neighboring Henrico County, Virginia found the unoccupied vehicle in a raggedy multi-housing complex known as Suburban Apartments. Authorities decided to covertly surveil the automobile, hoping that the suspects would return. It wasn't long before two men approached the Pathfinder. The men each had a full gasoline can in their hand. Police apprehended Andre Graham and Mark Sheppard, which prevented them from destroying evidence by setting the automobile on fire.

As police were putting together their case against Andre Graham, they learned that Mark Arlo Sheppard had been with Graham at the Steak & Ale murder. Sheppard was 22-years old at the time of the murders, and had a history of violence reaching back to when he was nine-years-old. Under questioning, Sheppard admitted to being at the scene of both the Stack and Rosenbluth murders. He told police that Andre Graham had been the triggerman in the killing of all three victims.

Sheppard said he had sold cocaine to the Rosenbluth couple on numerous occasions. He advised that the husband and wife owed him a lot of money. He testified that he and two partners, Andre Graham, and the third man, had gone to the Rosenbluth home. Mark Sheppard's fingerprints were found in 61 different places, which confirmed that he had indeed been inside the Rosenbluth residence.

It was later learned that Mark Sheppard was considered a probable suspect in about 10 other murders in the Richmond metro area. Sheppard was convicted of capital murder regarding Richard and Rebecca Rosenbluth, and sentenced to death by a Chesterfield jury. His convictions and sentences were affirmed on direct appeal before the Supreme Court of Virginia. He was executed by lethal injection at the Greenville Correctional Center on January 20, 1999.

Andre Graham

Andre Graham was ultimately convicted of the double murders of the Chesterfield County couple, and of the slaying of Sheryl Stack. After exhausting all appeals, his death sentence was carried out by lethal injection on 12-9-1999 at Greensville Correctional Center.

Story Behind The Story

Warden, You May Proceed with the Execution

Societal reprimand for wrongdoing is recorded in the earliest documentation of human history. The need to deal with illicit criminal behavior has led every civilization to implement punishment concepts that have varied greatly from culture to culture. A death sentence at the hands of the government is relatively rare; however, the ultimate parliamentary penalty for bad behavior has been imposed upon countless people over thousands of years.

Early executions around the world most often involved beatings, drowning, stoning, impalement, burning alive, poisoning, and crucifixion. Two of the most infamous judicial killings in early history include famed Greek Philosopher Socrates, who was forced to drink poison in 399 BC, and Jesus Christ of Nazareth, who was crucified in 29 ADS near Jerusalem.

Executions in North America

Colonizers from England brought the practice of capital punishment with them as they settled in Colonial America. Virginia became the first known English-speaking government in the new world to kill a resident when it executed George Kendall in 1608 for the crime of spying for Spain (Frost, 2018). Condemned colonists could find themselves facing a firing squad, beheaded by guillotine, burned at the stake, drawn and quartered, boiled in burning water, or hung from scaffolding.

In early American history, executions were public events. Large crowds would come from all around to witness the deaths. The 1853 hanging of John Wormeley in Chesterfield, Virginia drew a crowd that was said to be in excess of 4,000 people (LesCault, 2012). More famous felons in other parts of the country are said to have drawn throngs in the tens of thousands.

The largest communal execution in the U.S occurred in 1862 following the war between the U.S. and the Dakota Nation. Three hundred (300) Santee Sioux Indians were sentenced to death. President Abraham Lincoln ultimately commuted all but 39 of the sentences. One other Sioux was ultimately spared, but 38 Native Americans were hung in a mass execution (History.com., 2009).

In a strange twist of fate, on July 7, 1865, conspirators in the killing of President Abraham Lincoln were hanged in front of a crowd of only 1,000 invitees. Observers to the execution of the conspirators <u>were required to possess an invitation</u> from the government (Ruane, 2015). Chosen witnesses included family members of the accused, government employees, members of the armed forces, reporters, and selected representatives of the general public (Ruane, 2015).

End of Public Executions in the United States

The last person executed legally in America by public spectacle was 26-year-old Rainey Bethea (Dunden, 2018). Bethea was convicted of the rape and murder of a 70-year-old woman in Owensboro, Kentucky. Court records and photographs indicate that more than 20,000 people from around the Country attended the hanging. Publicity surrounding the festival like conditions at Bethea's demise prompted widespread calls to end lawful public killings.

Executions Behind Prison Wall

In 1938, Kentucky became the last State to ban public executions in the United States (Ryan 2001). Since that time, State sanctioned killings have become a combination of public and private undertakings. Private in the sense that lawful executions in America today take place behind prison walls. Public in essence because witnesses are allowed to be present; and, because media is called upon to convey pertinent information to the general population.

In 2020, 29 States and 55 independent countries consent to legal executions (Amnesty International Global Report 2019). Every American state has slightly different laws; however, all participating states allow some combination of witnesses with the following qualifications:

- Medical personnel
- Relatives of the condemned
- Spiritual advisors
- Relatives of the victim(s)
- Prison officials
- Private citizens
- Media representatives

The guillotine and Cyanide gas have been used as U.S. killing methods. Until recently, the majority of contemporary American municipal executions took the form of hanging, firing squad, or use of the electric chair.

Cruel and Unusual Punishment Ruling

In 1972, the Supreme Court of the United States ruled that state-run executions were unconstitutional. A majority of the court held that American execution methods amounted to cruel and unusual punishment, a violation of the 8th Amendment to the Constitution. No condemned prisoners were executed over the next 4-years. However, in 1976, the Court reversed its own decision and allowed government killings to resume.

As a result of this Supreme Court ruling, States began to contemplate more humanitarian considerations regarding condemned prisoners. Factors such as age, mental capacity, and literacy gained prominence during the death penalty phase of a trial. In 2005, the U.S. Supreme Court ruled that the execution of juvenile offenders was unconstitutional.

A desire for "more humane" methods of killing led to the concept of lethal injection. Death by lethal injection involves the administration of a combination of drugs to the inmate. Some believe that passive fatal drugs facilitate a more peaceful death. By 2020, nearly all government executions in America were carried out by lethal injection.

Last Meals and Last Words

The opportunity for condemned prisoners to make a statement immediately prior to their execution is an enduring element of the execution process (Johnson, 2014). Last words as part of putting the condemned to death can be traced to at least 1388 in England (Johnson, 2014). The final statement gives prisoners an opportunity to make an apology to their victims, or to declare their innocence one last time (Fuchs, 2013). Last words are recorded by officials. As many as 25% of prisoners choose to offer no final remarks (Fuchs, 2013).

Most states, but not all, allow the death row prisoners to order a meal of their choosing just prior to their execution. Nobody really knows why this tradition was adopted, nor why it persists.

Some believe that the state offers a meal to demonstrate a level of compassion to the condemned (Fuchs, 2013). Others theorize that the ending meal has a Christian connation that resembles The Last Supper (Nasaw, 2011). Regardless of the reason, almost all participating states allow a final meal. Not surprisingly, few inmates actually consume the final meal that is provided.

Right or Wrong

Death as a punishment at the order of the government, has always been highly controversial. One side passionately believes that the killing of one human being by another is morally repugnant, thus unequivocally unacceptable. Another segment of society believes just as fervently that capital punishment upholds the rule of law and serves as a significant deterrent to criminal behavior. Many others find themselves torn between the two rigid viewpoints.

My Eyes have Seen the Administration of Justice

The case studies identified below involve one defendant showcased in this book (Sniper John Muhammed), and one (Eric Payne) autonomous defendant not featured. The procedures used in both capital punishment cases, and the witness experiences are remarkably similar to what occurred during the execution of Andre Graham and Mark Shepard.

John Allen Muhammad (Witnessed by Jon Burkett)

The beltway sniper ordered chicken, red sauce, and cake for his last meal. However, after the meal was prepared and delivered, he chose not to eat. When asked by the warden if he had any last words, Muhammad chose not to speak.

The condemned man was dressed in denim jeans and a blue shirt. Constrained by shackles on his hands and his feet, he shuffled slowly into the death chamber. An eerie feeling permeated the witness compartment. A room designed for twelve (12) witnesses was overflowing as at least twenty-five (25) people crammed into metal chairs in the 24' by 24' space behind mirrored glass.

The walking dead man was surrounded by several state officials including the warden of the prison. At least six correctional officers would place the home-grown terrorist on a gurney. They proceeded to strap him to the gurney with leather buckles at his ankles, wrists, chest, and forehead.

A nurse started IV lines in both wrists so that the process of administering lethal drugs could begin. The warden asked firmly "do you have anything to say for the crimes that you have been convicted of committing?" Muhammad replied with a firm and almost defiant, "No."

The lethal injection process began. Witnesses were told that the lethal cocktail had been mixed and was ready for distribution. Three IV lines fed thru a blue curtain into the two IV systems attached to Muhammad's arms. In the briefing room earlier, corrections officials told the witnesses that they will know when the drugs are going into the body as two clear vials would make a slight bumping movement off of the curtain. Sure enough, you could see the nudge of the curtain. Muhammad's body was overtaken by the deadly dose.

The eyelids of the terrorist began to blink at a rapid pace. His breathing became quicker. His chest was rising and falling at a rapid pace. His eyelids were twitching, and his feet started to show signs of tension. Gradually, his breathing would become slower and more labored.

At 2111 hours, the warden picked up the phone and pronounced to the Governor's office that John Allen Muhammad was dead;

9:11 p.m. – what are the odds? September 9, 2001, is a date forever etched in American history when foreign terrorists hijacked planes and flew then into the World Trade Center. Nine-eleven, the day more than 3000 Americans were killed by foreign terrorists, would now also be associated with the death of a domestic terrorist who was responsible for killing as many as sixteen (16) strangers.

Muhammad was covered with a white sheet. Two tiny spots of blood could be seen on each wrist where the IV would be removed. Everybody in the witness room was escorted out to a passenger van that would be waiting in an enclosed courtyard surrounded by razor wire. The job of the media representative who witnessed the execution would be to give a statement about what happened inside the death chamber.

Eric Christopher Payne (Witnessed by Mindy Applewhite – Retired Deputy Chief Department of Corrections)

26-year-old Eric Payne was sentenced to death for sexually assaulting and killing two women with a hammer in 1997. At his sentencing, the trial judge likened Payne to a mad dog. Payne himself said that it would be best for all if he were put to death. Payne told his attorney that he would not participate in any appeals. Eric Payne went from sentencing to execution quicker than any inmate in the history of the state of Virginia.

Department of Corrections Deputy Chief Mindy Applewhite arrived early at the Greensville prison. Prison officials provided dinner for their high-ranking witness. After dinner, all witnesses were taken to the death sentence viewing room. Eric Payne ordered a final meal of sausage pizza, French fries, and sweet tea. It is not known whether Payne actually consumed his final meal.

As a Deputy Chief in the DOC, Mindy Applewhite was given the VIP circuit special. She actually sat in the electric chair. DOC employees showed her the drugs used for lethal injection, and explained how the fatal drugs would be administered.

Deputy Chief Applewhite chose to view the execution in the same room as the other legal witnesses. There was a red phone on the wall. The head of the Department of Corrections stood next to this phone. His singular task at the moment was to stand by the phone in case the condemned man changed his mind at the last second, and requested a stay of execution.

Eric Payne was brought into the execution chamber, strapped to a gurney. Prison guards checking the restraints (to make certain that they were tight) invoked a particularly vivid emotional reaction from the witnesses. Prison officials then closed the curtain. After a few minutes, the curtain reopened. Payne had the intravenous (IV) line in, and his hands were taped down.

When Deputy Chief Applewhite asked why Payne's hands had been taped down, a guard told her that the restraint was put in place to prevent the condemned man from "giving the finger" to witnesses. A witness next to the Deputy Chief stated that she saw Payne's heart "Almost jump out of his skin." The attending doctor indicated that the witness had seen how the body reacts to the administration of the lethal drugs.

Deputy Chief Applewhite saw the curtains between the viewing room and the execution chamber close again. When they re-opened, Eric Payne was gone. She remembers that the room smelled of alcohol and cleaning supplies. Mindy Applewhite said that she thought "Not much to it, he died more humanly than his victims did."

CHAPTER **11**

The Briley Brothers

MECKLENBURG CORRECTIONAL CENTER, VA
1984, Steve Neal and Jon Burkett know the case well.

Escape from Death Row

All hell broke loose in Virginia on May 31, 1984. Six death row inmates, regarded symbolically as the meanest of the mean, escaped from the maximum-security prison known as Mecklenburg Correctional Center. The escape plot was put in motion when

Linwood Briley, James Briley, Lemuel Tuggle, Earl Clanton, Derick Peterson, and Willie Jones overpowered guards in their prison pod. The inmates literally took over the death row unit.

During the coup d'état, both Briley brothers expressed strong interest in sexually assaulting the female staff and killing the captured guards that had been taken hostage. The Briley brothers discussed burning the guards alive by dousing them with rubbing alcohol. Other death row inmates stepped in and prevented the Briley brothers from murdering the guards and attacking the female employees.

It was disclosed during their subsequent trial, that the inmates had noticed that the correctional officers had become complacent in following procedures. Inmate Earl Clanton hid in an officer restroom waiting for just the right opportunity. When he felt that the time was right, Clanton sprang into action, hoodwinking the unsuspecting prison guard. More details of the takeover and kidnapping of the guard will be found in the *Story Behind the Story* segment that follows this report.

The cunning death row inmates had planned their escape well. The prisoners donned stolen guard uniforms and covered their faces with pilfered riot helmets. The prisoners insinuated to authorities that they had a bomb. As proof of their assertion, they covered a small tv with a blanket, and put it on a stretcher. The inmates hastily ran through the prison, spraying the bomb with a fire extinguisher. They made their way to a waiting Correctional Department van. The inmates quickly commandeered the van, and recklessly drove right out of the front gate of the maximum-security prison. The most daring death row escape in Virginia history was in-progress.

On the Run

The inmates quickly abandoned the Dept. of Corrections van just across the North Carolina state line. The search apparatus assembled by law enforcement was colossal. Hundreds of officers from throughout the region were massed and deployed to hunt for the escapees. Resources were instantaneously gobbled up in both Virginia and North Carolina.

The intensive search went non-stop throughout the night. The following day an officer on patrol spotted two men inside a small laundromat in North Carolina. Earl Clanton and Derick Peterson were inside the laundromat eating cheese and drinking cheap wine. Their capture meant that law enforcement had two bad guys back in custody, but there were still four more on the lam.

Stole a Truck and Headed North

Law enforcement continued to comb the region. With each passing minute the threat to the public became more worrisome. Hour after hour, local and Federal law enforcement continued their desperate search. All investigative means (family connections, aerial surveillance, covert operations, aquatic surveillance, electronic data mining, etc.) were fully operational. Law enforcement theorized that the killers would be looking for a way to escape the area.

It wasn't long before law enforcement intuition became reality. A couple in the area notified police that their personal vehicle (truck) had been stolen from their driveway during the middle of the night. Knowing that the prisoners were very likely mobile meant that some of the outlaws could be in the Richmond metropolitan region, threatening our residents. Though unknown for certain, law enforcement suspected that due to family connections, the inmates would head north on I-95 in the stolen truck. Once again, the authorities were right on the money.

Four Escapees Split Up

Linwood and James Briley were dropped off at a relative's home in Philadelphia, Pennsylvania. Lem Tuggle and Willie Jones continued on toward Canada. In Vermont, Tuggle and Jones used the stolen truck to commit a robbery. A Vermont State trooper spotted the truck and gave chase. Lem Tuggle was apprehended shortly thereafter. Willie Jones gave himself up the following day.

Capture of the Briley Brothers

 Law enforcement was relieved that four of the six escapees were now back in custody. However, the most dangerous of the group, Lin-  wood and James Briley, were still at large. Investigative leads caused law enforce- ment to believe the brothers may have been hiding in the Phila- delphia area. A Federal judge authorized a phone intercept on the home of a Briley relative. Following a traced phone call, heavily armed authorities raided this relative's home. SWAT teams exerted overpowering force as they took the treacherous Briley brothers back into custody.

Why the Briley Brothers Were on Death Row

Linwood Briley, James Briley, and Anthony Briley grew up in the Highland Park neighborhood in Richmond, Virginia. It has been widely reported that the Briley parents were intensely afraid of their blood offspring. Neighbors indicated that the Briley boys were known to be infatuated with exotic pets such as tarantulas, piranhas, and boa constrictors. All of the Briley boys had a history of criminal activity from a young age. Linwood Briley committed his first murder at the age of 16. James Briley was institutionalized at 16 for shooting at a police officer during a pursuit.

By 1979, The Briley brothers and friend Duncan Meekins were leading a frenzied crime spree in RVA. In March, a 21-year-old vending machine serviceman was assaulted, murdered, and robbed in his suburban home. Two weeks later, 76-year-old women was raped and murdered. A couple of months went by before a 17-year-old male was abducted, and dragged into a nearby backyard. He was killed when a cinderblock was smashed over his head.

Intense fear and panic mounted as the terror lingered. On September 14, a disc jockey performing with his band at the Satellite nightclub on Jefferson Davis Highway was abducted, driven out to Mayo Island, shot dead, and dumped into the James River. Linwood Briley was wearing this victim's ring when he was arrested. Two-weeks later, a 62-year-old female was beaten to death with a baseball bat during a home invasion. Five days after that incident, a 79-year-old female and her 59-year-old boarder were bludgeoned to death during another home invasion.

On October 19, a longtime associate of the brothers and his girlfriend were found dead in their home. Both victims were bound, gagged with duct tape, and shot in the head. The female had been raped.

The Briley brothers and Duncan Meekins were eventually identified as suspects by police. Law enforcement hypothesized that Meekins was the gang's weakest link, and offered him a plea agreement

Duncan Meekins

to disclose his knowledge of the crimes. Meekins took the deal. His confession provided complete details regarding the deadly six-month crime binge. Meekins was ultimately convicted and incarcerated, but spared the death penalty due to his cooperation. Anthony Briley was also convicted and incarcerated, but spared the death penalty because it was found that he was not considered the "triggerman" during any of the homicides.

Executions

Linwood Briley was executed in the electric chair at the Virginia State Penitentiary in Richmond on October 12, 1984.

James Briley was executed in the electric chair at the Virginia State Penitentiary in Richmond on April 18, 1985.

The other four inmates involved in the infamous death row escape were also executed by the State of Virginia.

Earl Clanton
Executed April 14, 1988

Derick Peterson
Executed Aug. 22, 1991

Willie Leroy Jones
Executed Sept. 11, 1992

Lem Tuggle
Executed Dec. 12, 1996

Story Behind the Story

My Guardian Angel(s)

Death row is a nasty place. A hell hole where the worst criminals await judgment day, an interval that can sometimes take years if not decades. Prisoners have nothing but never-ending time to think, sometimes fantasizing over what it would be like to once again be free. Everything is in play as guards check on the caged monsters that await mortality. Many of the inmates on death row are vile, nasty, and often callous human beings with a moral compass whose arrow is stuck on south, symbolic of where their souls will rot.

Coraleen Thomas Epps was raised a law-and-order sort of gal in Mecklenburg County, Virginia. Her father, John Lewis "Rock" Thomas was the first African-American police officer in South Hill, Virginia. Following a stellar 27-year career, and nearly three decades after his death, Rock Thomas' highly respected name still fondly rolls off the tongues of old timers in that rural part of the State.

Coraleen said that her dad "Knew everyone, was a good listener, and that he was known to give great advice." Ms. Epps says that Rock Thomas "Had a way with people, knew how to talk with people, he was a strong role model." He sang, danced, and was in the church choir. "He was my heart" said Coraleen. Not surprisingly, Rock's daughter wanted to follow her father into law enforcement. In 1981, Rock Thomas helped his daughter obtain a job with the Virginia Department of Corrections.

Coraleen Thomas went to work at the Mecklenburg Correctional Center in Boydton, Virginia as a prison guard. She worked either in the tower, or in the control room at various prison buildings. At the time, the Department of Corrections (DOC) utilized their employees (male & female guards) as interchangeable parts.

Even though there were no female inmates at Mecklenburg, Coraleen said that "When you applied, you applied as a correctional officer. Sex [Gender] wasn't anything in it. You were a correctional officer. You worked wherever you were assigned." Coraleen was qualified with a handgun, a shotgun, and the M-16 rifle. "I didn't feel unsafe," she said.

May 31, 1984

Coraleen's favorite job assignment was working in the tower. However, on the historic 4 -12 shift, she was assigned to work in the control room of building #1. Her duty that summer night consisted of controlling the doors to the guard room. The death row pod wasn't physically any different than the others. What made it unique was that Building #1 housed the condemned killers. Coraleen had worked death row previously, and her workday started routinely.

Coraleen recalls other guards transporting an inmate with a heart condition for treatment. As the inmate passed by her in the control room, she recollects noticing that the inmate gave her a very strange look. Coraleen says that she didn't pay much attention to it at the time, but she later learned that this same inmate had been asked to participate in the escape. Looking back on it now, she is convinced that the sick prisoner was trying to forewarn her that something sinister was afoot.

Coraleen stated that at the time of the escape, "They were doing a lot of hiring at the prison. Turnover was bad, new hires would come and go before you really learned who you were working alongside. You often couldn't put a face to fellow employees because so many were new," she said.

Approximately halfway through her shift, a guard approached Coraleen's control room and indicated that he needed to get in. A clean cut and crisply dressed man in a correctional uniform firmly said, "Thomas, I need you to open the door and let me in." Even though she didn't immediately recognize the man, "He looked like a guard." Coraleen pressed the button to let who she thought was a fellow employee into the control room.

When the "guard" entered the control room, he immediately overpowered Coraleen. "He held a shank to my throat." For those who may be unfamiliar, a shank is a homemade knife that prisoners forge from prison materials. "I realized then that it was an inmate executing a plan to escape and doing it with precision," Coraleen said. The subduing prisoner, Earl Clanton, said to me, "I need you to come into the bathroom and stay on your knees. And that is exactly what I did," said Coraleen.

Live or Die

Earl Clanton asked for a verbal tutorial regarding which buttons to push to open the doors. The other inmates had come down by that time. "I told him which buttons to push. He let them [other inmates] out. I could hear them coming into the control room, and I really got scared." She knew that two of the convicts were the Briley brothers. "They were ruthless," Coraleen said, "They didn't care what they did."

Coraleen said that she could hear rustling outside the bathroom door, but that she was unable to make out what the inmates were talking about. She said "I went blank, stricken with fear. The only thing I could think. OMG, they are going to rape me, was my first thought. I didn't cry, but I was really scared. Shock, and disbelief that this was happening, and that I was involved in it."

Escapee Clanton "Told me to stay calm, that he wasn't going to hurt me. I said, please don't hurt me, I just had a baby." Clanton said to Coraleen, "I'm not going to let anybody come in here and hurt you, I have children too." He stood at the door, never allowing any other inmates to enter the bathroom. Clanton ordered Coraleen to tell him which buttons to push at the control panel. This permitted the opening of the doors, which allowed the prisoners to get out of the building.

Minutes felt like hours as Epps stayed down in a position that was similar to praying bedside. Coraleen recalls that her mind was focused on, "If I am killed, I would be leaving my baby without a parent. That was my biggest thought," she said. Her mindset was singularly focused upon "I have a child, you can leave, *just let me live*. Until you are in that situation, you don't know what you are going to do," said Coraleen.

Earl Clanton opened the doors and the escapees fled to a waiting van. They used a stretcher and a fire extinguisher to make it appear as though they had a bomb. They made it clear that they would detonate the device if anyone attempted to interfere with their escape. In response to the bomb threat, a second female guard opened the front gate of the prison allowing the escapees to drive away.

Life Impact for the Strong Lady Survivor

Back in the mid 1980's, the law enforcement profession didn't know much about Post Traumatic Stress Disorder (PTSD). Coraleen recalls that the Department of Corrections "Didn't offer us anything, no counseling, nothing." They did require her to take a lie detector test, and she left the job. Her father, Rock Thomas, made it clear to his girl that "You don't want that, you're not going back" when there was a possibility of her returning to work at the prison.

Coraleen recalls that the timeframe following her traumatic ordeal was rough on her and her family. "Nerves got the better of me," she said. "I started going off on family." She saw a medical Doctor who helped her with medication. Coraleen admiringly recalls how Rock Thomas again stepped in to help his daughter. "He gave me some money, telling me to leave town for a few days, to get myself together."

Even to this day, Coraleen says that she is very leery when she goes out. She said that she constantly watches her surroundings. She still finds it hard to believe that she actually survived her life-threatening nightmare. Her five children are amazed that their mom was actually part of one of the greatest death row escapes in U.S. history.

Three Guardian Angels

Coraleen instinctively understands that the way in which she was raised likely played a huge role in her survival. Mom and Dad "Raised us that you treat people the way that you want to be treated. If I hadn't been friendly with some of the inmates, just saying hi," Coraleen said. "Earl Clanton used to speak to me thru the window as I was going to my building. I didn't treat him as an inmate; I spoke, you know, just being decent. Hey, they are criminals, but they are also human beings. They gave me respect, so I gave them respect back."

When asked if she thought that respect was why Clanton had protected her during the escape, she said, "I think so." After the escapees were recaptured, all 6 were eventually put to death by the State of Virginia. Coraleen said that she prayed for Earl Clanton before and after his date with his maker. His execution impacted her deeply. "I felt really sorry," she said. "He protected me, and he didn't have to. It really saddened me when they killed him."

Coraleen made it clear that she feels as though the good Lord was watching over her. It is amazing how her faith in God, Rock Thomas, and the unlikely Earl Clanton all worked together to ensure that the young Thomas girl survived the historic prison escape of 1984.

CHAPTER **12**

She Just Showed Up

*RICHMOND, VA 1987, Jon Burkett and Steve Neal
know the case well.*

Regrettably, Chesterfield County, Virginia has a long and sordid history of child abduction cases. Some of the more notable cases involve the still unsolved 1974 abduction, rape, and murder of 7-year-old Christie Wright in the Chester Town House Apartments. Another famous dreadful assault on a child occurred in 1987, when an 8-year-old girl was abducted, raped, stabbed, and left to die. Franz Henry Dejong was arrested and incarcerated for that repulsive crime. Everett Lee Mueller was executed in Virginia's death chamber for the 1990 kidnapping, rape, and homicide of 10-year-old Charity Powers. Sadly, there are many more.

Afternoon Bus Stop Abduction

The innocent children of the County saw inexcusable evil visited upon them once again in the fall of 1987. Late in the afternoon, a young mother frantically called police to report that her 7-year-old daughter had not come home from school. The parents stated that their latchkey daughter was supposed to go straight home in the Three Pines subdivision after she got off the school bus.

The first protocol for any missing child case is to thoroughly search the interior and exterior of the child's home. When these searches produced negative results, police checked the missing girl's last known location, A.M. Davis Elementary School. Police also confirmed that the young girl was not with any known relatives or friends. A brownie girl scout meeting was scheduled for later that evening, so police verified that she was not at the church for the scout meeting.

No-one familiar to the child had seen or heard from her. As police continued to investigate the disappearance, a neighborhood canvas yielded some disturbing new clues.

Upon questioning, more than one child at the Mountain Pine Boulevard and Spruce Pine Drive bus stop reported seeing the missing girl get into a blue Ford Bronco type of vehicle immediately after getting off the school bus. Though their descriptions were what one would  expect from elementary age children, the witnesses said that there was a male with red hair inside the suspicious Bronco.

Missing Girl Walks into Her Brownie Scout Meeting

Roughly 3-hours into the investigation, an odd phone call unexpectedly came into the police communications center. The brownie girl scout leader whom police had talked with earlier, called dispatch and said, "She just showed up." Strangely, out of the blue, the missing 7-year-old girl walked into the church where her scout meeting was about to begin.

Investigation

After checking her physical well-being, a Detective interviewed the girl. The victim initially told police that nothing unusual had occurred with her that day. After being carefully and skillfully pressed, the 7-year-old stated that a man that she did not know had taken her to a McDonalds restaurant after school. She further advised that the man had driven her around for a long time, and that they had stopped at a drive-thru bank to get money.

The missing girl also told the Detective that she and the man had gone to "some people's house" in the country, and that the man had instructed her to act as if she was his daughter. The victim said that she told the abductor about her girl scout meeting, so the "Man dropped me off" at the door of the church where the meeting was to take place.

Those familiar with child sexual assault cases know that an interviewer must be very careful not to "lead" or manipulate a child victim into making a statement that is not factual. Even though the second grader in this case did not describe anything further, the detective strongly suspected that a sexual assault had occurred. The detective looked into the victim's school bookbag. Inside the bookbag were underwear and a t-shirt that the girl's mother indicated she was wearing when she left for school earlier that morning. The detective's heart sank, because though the 7-year-old had not stated it, he was now virtually certain that something sexually reprehensible had happened to this young child.

Intense media attention raised awareness and put families in the area on high alert. Detectives worked tirelessly on the case with little success. Day after day, still the only suspect information available was a man with red hair driving a blue Ford Bronco type of vehicle.

Not Another One

Less than 2-miles away, and just a few weeks after the Mountain Pine Boulevard kidnapping, it happened again! Chesterfield Emergency Communications Center 911 lines were lighting up! Numerous callers in the Foxberry subdivision were reporting the forcible abduction of a young child shortly after she got off the school bus. Police arrived to find panicked parents and several child witnesses.

The elementary school witnesses relayed very similar stories. It turns out that the bus had stopped to disembark students as usual. Child witnesses advised that a man with red hair and glasses grabbed the 9-year-old victim in the street and forcibly drug her into a white sedan type vehicle before driving away. No license information was known, and the description of the suspect was limited.

Detectives immediately recognized the possibility that the two cases were very likely related. Due to the late afternoon hour, Detectives made a decision to ask the local news media for help. Media assembled quickly, and before long a Detective was on TV providing details about the cases.

After completing the TV interview, the Detectives resumed obtaining information from the 2nd victim's parents. Suddenly, out of no-where, the screaming 9-year-old girl burst through the front door of her own home. Everyone, including the police, were STUNNED! The tearful, yet joyous reunion in the family living room of her home is one that this detective will never forget.

During their interview with the 9-year-old, Detectives learned that the girl had been kidnapped, driven a long way "in the country," and that she had been forcibly sexually assaulted. The girl stated that the male suspect with red hair and glasses drove her back to her neighborhood and dropped her off near her home after the assault. Once free, the victim said that she ran straight home.

Just in Case

While Detectives interviewed the victim, police communications received a phone call from a man who lived in the same Foxberry neighborhood. The man had seen portions of the live, on-scene, 6 p.m. newscast interview. The man advised of a suspicious situation that he had observed in the neighborhood earlier in the day. He called to tell police about what he had seen.

Detectives immediately responded to the adult witness' home. The man and his family were seated around the dinner table. The man told Detectives that earlier in the afternoon, he had been working underneath his car in his driveway. The witness noticed a man sitting in a white automobile on the street. Thinking that it was odd, the witness used a nail to scratch the vehicle license plate into a piece of plywood, "just in case." Detectives took possession of the small cutout of plywood with a Virginia license number prominently displayed. More details of this hero witness and his actions will be found in the *Story Behind the Story* segment that follows this report.

The Suspect and the Arrest

In checking the license plate number from the plywood board, detectives learned that the registered owner of the vehicle lived in rural Powhatan County, Virginia. His physical descriptors included a notation that he had red hair and that he wore prescription glasses. Later that night, detectives drove to the address listed for the vehicle. The registrants long and winding driveway extended well off the roadway. When the detectives got near the house, they found a blue Bronco and a white sedan sitting side by side in the driveway. The two Detectives glanced at each other, each thinking, BINGO! The investigation suddenly resembled an operational microwave oven, red hot heat generated in mere seconds.

Upon knocking at the suspect's door, the wife advised that her husband was in the bed asleep. The Detectives told the wife, "You need to get him up, we want to talk with him." A red-haired man with glasses soon emerged from the hallway. One look, **the direct eye contact,** convinced Detectives that they were looking at the vile suspect. The suspect agreed to voluntarily accompany the Detectives to the Powhatan Sheriff's office for questioning.

Confession and Arrest

Thomas A. McMillan provided a full confession to the abduction and sexual assault of both girls. He identified the location "In the country" (Powhatan County) where the sexual assaults had taken place. He confirmed the younger victim's account regarding the stop at a McDonald's and at a bank-teller machine. McMillan admitted that he had gotten his vehicle stuck in the mud during the first sexual assault, and that he had sought help from the owners of the closest house to his location. Detectives were able to confirm with a local couple in Powhatan that McMillan and a small girl had actually been to their home asking for assistance on the night of the first crime.

Thomas Anthony McMillan, 31, who had no prior criminal history, was arrested on the spot and incarcerated with no bond. He was charged with two (2) counts of forcible abduction with intent to defile, and two (2) counts of aggravated sexual battery upon a minor. According to testimony at his sentencing, McMillan had been drinking heavily and using cocaine and marijuana in both cases. McMillan's wife, Connie, testified that her husband had been under pressure at his job at Philip Morris and that he had undergone a change in the past year that affected his behavior. "He was just wild," Connie McMillan said.

He was convicted and sentenced to 60-years in prison. McMillian, a registered sex offender, is incarcerated Inmate # 1094258 at the Dillwyn Correctional Center at the time of this writing.

Story Behind The Story

Gut Wrenching Heroism

Gut instinct is a characteristic that every human possesses. Some have stronger sensations than others; nevertheless, it is part of our DNA that steers people towards doing what is morally right. "Trust your gut" is more than a cliché for Brent Hodges. His strong occupational ethic had him backed into a corner in late 1987. The end of the year was coming, and Mr. Hodges had unused vacation time at work. Either use it, or lose it.

Two innocent families in Central Virginia had no way of knowing that the loss of labor for Brent's employer would be a godsend for their flesh and blood. Faith in his instincts would transform Brent Hodges' into a spot-on rescuer. A Friday away from work would help a good citizen solve two kidnapping cases and put a child predator behind bars.

Working on his Day Off

Like most hard-working Americans, Brent Hodges was determined to make the most of his day off. He had a few chores to complete. By mid-afternoon, he was outside working odd jobs in the yard, and taking care of things around the house. First on his list, was to change the oil in his car. He gathered supplies: oil, filter, wrench, and an old piece of plywood to lay on the ground so he wouldn't muddy his clothes. "I kept seeing this car go by," Brent said. "Initially, I didn't think that it was extraordinarily unusual."

He Just Didn't Look Right

After watching the vehicle loop around his neighborhood like a vulture circling to pluck meat from the carcass of a deer left for dead in the ditch, Hodges internal radar started going off. He noticed that the same small white vehicle had stopped about 75-feet from his home. The man behind the wheel was just sitting in the car by himself. Hodges had a gut feeling; the man with the carrot top was up to no good.

The automobile sat still for about ten-minutes. Brent stated, "Something told me that he wasn't right." He recalls that he felt like it would be a good idea to make a note of the car's license plate, "Just in case." Since he was underneath his own vehicle in his driveway, Brent Hodges had no pen or paper. Trying to be inconspicuous, he felt around, determined to find a way to document the suspicious license plate. His fingers fumbled until he came across a nail. He took the nail and scratched the license plate number of the white car into the piece of plywood that he was laying on.

After just a few minutes, the car pulled away from its temporary street parking spot. "That was the last that I thought of it," Brent recalled. "Later, I saw him pass back by with a child in the front seat who did not appear to be in obvious distress." At that point Brent shrugged it off, thinking, "Okay, he was just waiting for a child to pick up." The board that he had etched the license number was put away at the rear of his home.

Hours later, Hodges was continuing his list of chores. As the roar of the vacuum cleaner reverberated throughout his home, he looked up and saw an image on television that grabbed his attention. It was video from the 6 o'clock newscast. Brent said that he "Didn't hear, but I glanced over and, on the screen, they had a picture of our sign." The image he saw was the Foxberry subdivision entrance sign flashing across the screen. Curious, and thinking, "What the heck," Brent turned off the vacuum and started watching the news story.

Police were holding a press conference about a child abduction that had taken place in the Foxberry subdivision. Brent vividly recalls contemplating, "**WHOA**, I think I know who that was!" He immediately dialed 911, knowing that he had something that could help police find the red-headed suspect. Brent remembers that someone in authority called him back and asked him if he meant to call the Crime Solvers (tip line) number. He said, "No, not really, because I knew that this was something that needed immediate attention."

While awaiting the arrival of law enforcement, Brent told his wife, Cindy, what he had observed. He then went outside and retrieved the plywood board. He cut the piece of the board that contained the etched license number. He had "Scratched that board with all I had," Brent recalls. When Detectives arrived at the Hodges' residence, Brent handed them the 2 by 6-inch plywood cutout.

The Alert Witness Broke the Case

You will recall from our crime story in this chapter that law enforcement had very little suspect information in these cases. The witnesses in both cases were young kids. The information that they provided to police was in good faith, but the quality of the data was precisely what you would expect from little children.

A male with glasses and red hair who had been driving a blue Bronco and a small white car. That is the full extent of the suspect information known at the time. Though they were working the cases with all their mite, solving these two kidnappings would have been impossible without the keen eye and well-founded instincts of Brent Hodges.

When asked what it was that caused him to get involved, Brent Hodges said, "I don't mind calling [the police]. I saw him a lot, he was going slow, and I didn't recognize the car. Maybe the planets were aligned, at the time, *it wasn't right*," he said. "So many things fell into place that made this all happen. I happened to be off, I happened to be working in the yard. That night when the news was on, I happened to be in the living room. I happened to look up and saw the sign [on tv]."

Too Close to Home – Literally

At the time of this incident, Brent and Cindy had two very young children, one boy, and one girl. Another girl, and another boy would follow. The family continued to live in the Foxberry subdivision for the next 10-years. Brent said that he often thought of the child victims, especially as his own children grew. When he heard stories of something similar happening it would trigger going back to that day, Brent said. "I don't know what I would have done" if it had happened to my children.

Brent Hodges was interviewed several times by local media. He was recognized and commended by the Fraternal Order of Police (FOP), and he received accolades at a Chesterfield Police Department award ceremony. A local television station used his news interview to highlight and promote a "Crime Watch" program that encouraged citizens to be proactive against crime.

It is well known in the Public Safety arena that law enforcement can't solve all crimes by themselves. Thankfully, there are concerned citizens willing to get involved. Brent Hodges believes that God put him in place on that fateful day. It is almost certain that other little girls would have been abducted, sexually assaulted, or killed if the law-abiding resident had not intervened.

Decades later, there are a lot of parents thankful that Mr. Hodges followed his gut instincts. Though he said that he doesn't feel like a hero, Brent Hodges uttered what is perhaps the greatest of understatements when he said, "I knew it was important."

CHAPTER **13**

Murder "Mon"

RICHMOND, VA 2003, *Jon Burkett and Steve Neal*
know the case well.

A Surprise in the House

October 25, 2003, Police were called to "check the welfare" of a family at a house in the 7800 block of Bur Oak Lane in Chesterfield County, Virginia. Upon arrival to the Brentwood community (just north of Harry Daniel Park), law enforcement noticed no vehicles in the driveway. The yard was unkempt, the house was closed up, and it appeared that no-one was home. Police knocked at the door; a phone call inside failed to generate any response.

The concerned complainant and neighbors provided clues about the resident's drug dealing lifestyle that led police to suspect that something foul was afoot. When police forced entry into the residence, they found 32-year-old Tasha S. "Lady" Robinson shot to death in her bedroom. She had a gunshot wound to the back of the head, execution style. Police methodically cleared (tactical search to determine additional victims or threats) the home. Upstairs in a small bedroom, police found a 22-month-old male toddler in a crib. Miraculously, the baby was alive and unharmed.

Early Investigation

Every homicide case begins with a few key questions. Once answered, these background inquiries routinely provide a roadmap for the course of the investigation. The first fundamental set of questions for investigators are: who is the victim, what do they do, and with whom do they associate? The second group of key queries is: when did the crime occur, and what does our crime scene evidence tell us about what happened? Thirdly, why was the victim killed? In the Murder "Mon" situation, there was also a fourth vital piece of the initial puzzle; where were the other residents who lived in the victim's home?

As they began to peel the onion in this case, investigators quickly established that Lady Robinson had been living in the home for more than a year with her boyfriend and her two sons. The victim, nor her companion, Anthony Novedo Rankine, had any known source of legitimate income. Rankine, a Jamaican national, was rumored to be involved with international narcotics trafficking and organized crime in Jamaica. He was also believed to be running a very large marijuana distribution operation in the metropolitan Richmond area.

The forensic crime scene search furnished some noteworthy clues that helped law enforcement unravel the mystery. The execution style murder indicated that the killer(s) wanted to send a message. Additionally, Police discovered a safe in the home. Approximately $60,000 in cash was found undisturbed within the unprotected safe. The discovery of a large amount of money that *had not been stolen*, led police to suspect that burglary/robbery was not the intention of these murder suspects.

Crime scene indicators and background hints were conveying a loud and clear message to investigators. Drugs, and the illicit consequences that accompany that illegal lifestyle, were quickly coming into focus as the most likely motive for this homicide.

The last immediate issue at hand for quizzical investigators was: where is Anthony Rankine and Tasha's oldest son, 13-year-old Marquis Jobes? Why were they not in the home? Were they potentially the murder suspects? Had they fled the scene? Had they been kidnapped? Why had 22-month-old baby Mahkail Rankine been abandoned, alive and uninjured?

Amber Alert for Marquis Jobes

October 28, 2003, Police issued an Amber Alert for missing Marquis Jobes:

RICHMOND – Virginia State Police issued an Amber Alert Tuesday for a missing 13-year-old Chesterfield County boy.

Police said Marquis Jobes may be in "extreme danger,'" and could have been abducted by his mother's boyfriend, according to Chesterfield County police spokeswoman Ann Reid.

Jobes is described as black, about 5 feet tall and weighing 110 pounds. He has brown eyes and black hair. He has been missing since at least Saturday morning, when Jobes' mother, 32-year-old Tasha Robinson, was found shot to death in their home. Robinson's 22-month-old toddler was found unharmed in a crib.

Reid said Jobes could be in the company of 29-year-old Anthony Novedo Rankine, who lived in the home with Robinson. Rankine is suspected of having ties to international crime groups, police said.

Rankine is described as a black male, 5 feet 10 inches tall and weighing 160 pounds. He has brown eyes and black hair, and has scars on his head and chest.

Any information should be directed to the Virginia State Police at (800) 822-4453, or Chesterfield County Police at (804) 748-1832.

DEA Investigation and Press Release

Law enforcement began a deep dive into the life of Jamaican drug dealer Anthony Rankine and his associates. Regional partners with the Henrico Division of Police, Virginia State Police, Richmond Police Department, and the Virginia Capital Police provided valuable assistance in the investigation. Federal law enforcement partners from the DEA; the U.S. Attorney for the Eastern District of Virginia; the Bureau of Alcohol, Tobacco, Firearms, and Explosive's, the IRS Criminal Division; and the Federal Bureau of Investigation also joined the investigative team.

Investigators found that Rankine received 500-pound crates of marijuana at least twice a month from his suppliers on the west coast. It was reported that his organization kept its cash rubber-ban wrapped in $1,000 stacks. Law enforcement obtained warrants charging Rankine with possession of a firearm by a convicted felon, drug distribution, conspiracy, and immigration violations. Additional details surrounding the Drug dealing associated with this situation are catalogued in the *"Story Behind the Story"* segment that follows this crime case.

October 31, 2003, six-days after Tasha Robinson's murder, police arrested seven (7) men who had ties to Anthony Rankine. Marcel Lamont Hughes, Shannon Markus Bell, Hanlon Garth Eccleston, Raymond Floyd Barrett, Dashawn Andre Saunders, Rahmone Agustus Taylor, and Richard Dwight Bernard faced state charges involving drug-conspiracy-related offenses. Five of the seven were reportedly Jamaican Nationals.

Police seized a large quantity of marijuana, cash, weapons, as well as three vehicles, one of which Rankine was known to use. Police would drop these state charges when the suspects were later indicted on Federal drug charges.

Anthony Novedo Rankine Found Dead

November 5, 2003, Police were called to check on a rented white van (JER-5286) that had been abandoned in the parking lot of the Department of Motor Vehicles near Leigh Street in Richmond. Inside the van they discovered the decomposing remains of 29-year-old Anthony Rankine. Rankine had been shot in the back of his head, execution style. Investigators found a plastic bag over Rankine's head. His hands and feet were bound with duct tape. Decomposition of the body suggested that Rankine had been dead for at least a week, possibly longer.

Authorities connected Rankine's killing to a Henrico County, Virginia house. During a search at the address in the 3500 block of Ammons Avenue, police and federal agents found scales used for weighing drugs, blood on the floor, and bullet holes in a wall at the house. Police said publicly that the home was believed to have been used for distributing marijuana. Forensic tests were conducted on the blood found in the house in an attempt to determine who it belonged to, and whether it came from more than one person.

Marquis Jobes on America's Most Wanted

November 8, 2003, the nationally syndicated television show *America's Most Wanted* featured the case of missing teen Marquis Jobes. Law enforcement was pulling out all the stops in their effort to find Marquis.

Richard Dwight Bernard Indicted on Federal Drug Charges

November 2003, A Federal grand jury returned an indictment for Richard Dwight Bernard of Jacksonville, Arkansas, and Richmond, Virginia. Bernard, and the seven others were charged with conspiracy to distribute in excess of 1,000 kilograms of marijuana, and with possession of a firearm in furtherance of drug trafficking.

Marquis Jobes Found Dead

December 13, 2003, the search for the 13-year-old Jobes ended tragically. Police discovered the body of the missing Chesterfield County boy in woods behind a Kmart on Midlothian Turnpike in South Richmond. Authorities indicated that they had received information about the boy's possible whereabouts. Police used a cadaver dog to locate the body.

Marquis Jobes' remains were found in a drainage culvert about 100 feet inside the woods and scattered over a small area. Police hypothesized that the remains had been in the woods since the time of his disappearance, noting that they had been disturbed by weather conditions and wildlife.

April 20, 2004
Contact: SA Heath Anderson
Phone Number: 202-305-8500

FOR IMMEDIATE RELEASE

Superseding Indictment for Drug and Murder Charges

APR 20, 2004 – A federal grand jury returned a superseding indictment today for Richard Dwight Bernard, age 35, of Jacksonville, Arkansas and Richmond, Virginia. Bernard was originally charged in November 2003, along with seven others, with conspiracy to distribute in excess of 1,000 kilograms of marijuana and with possession of firearms in furtherance of a drug trafficking crime.

In February 2004, the indictment was amended to *add a charge* **alleging that Bernard, while engaging in the drug conspiracy, intentionally killed Anthony Rankine, Tasha Robinson, and Marquis Jobes, age 13, on October 22, 2003.** In addition, the indictment charges Bernard with using a firearm during and in relation to a drug trafficking crime. Each charge involving the murders of Rankine, Robinson, and Jobes carries a maximum sentence of life imprisonment and is death penalty eligible.

Assistant U.S. Attorneys Olivia N. Hawkins and Charles E. James, Jr. are prosecuting the case for the U.S. Attorney's Office. The following agencies provided valuable assistance in this investigation: Chesterfield Police Department, Henrico Police Department, State Department, Bureau of Immigrations and Customs Enforcement (BICE), Virginia State Police, Richmond Police Department, and the Virginia Capital Police.

Case Disposition

The Federal drug case against Bernard hinged upon the testimony of codefendants who flipped for the prosecution. Following his plea agreement, one codefendant served only 12-years as a result

of his deal with the government. He ended up going back to Jamaica following his release.

Murder charges regarding the killings of Tasha Robinson, Anthony Rankine, and Marquis Jobes were dropped by prosecutors when Bernard agreed to plead guilty to a Federal charge involving Conspiracy to Distribute more than 1000 kilos of marijuana, and possessing a firearm in furtherance of a drug trafficking crime. Bernard was sentenced to **life in prison plus 5-years** pursuant to his plea agreement with the government.

At the time of this writing, RICHARD DWIGHT BERNARD, Federal inmate # 38304-083 is incarcerated at Federal Correctional Institution Gilmer in Glenville, WV

Story Behind The Story

Tricked Out Stereo System

Organized Crime and International Drugs

Jamaica gained its independence from the United Kingdom in 1962. Many of the country's poor were living in large urban areas that often-lacked paved streets and basic sanitation (Grillo, 2014). Strongmen (local power brokers) known as "Dons" emerged, seized power, and took control in the ghettoes. The country's two major political parties, Jamaica Labor Party and People's National Party, both pursued support from the Dons. The Dons promised to deliver votes in exchange for money and development projects in their garrisons (Grillo 2014).

Not surprisingly, political corruption unleashed intense internal violence in Jamaica. Ferocious drug gangs, known as Posses, flourished locally. Over the years, the Posses began to export drugs abroad. Marijuana was grown in the Jamaican countryside, then smuggled on boats and cargo ships to Florida. From Florida, the drug was trafficked to other parts of the U.S. and beyond. The first Jamaican gangs were identified in the United States in Brooklyn, New York, in the 1970's (Volsky 1987).

Through the decades that followed, Posse members became well-known for their viciousness, showing little regard for public safety or human life. The Jamaican organized crime gangs were recognized for deadly retribution, ritualized murders of members who rip off profits on drugs (Grillo, 2014). In the early part of the 21st century, (when our Murder "Mon" case took place), The Shower

Posse, led by Christopher "Dudas" Coke, was masterminding the trafficking of tons of marijuana into the United States and around the world (USODC, 2005).

Everett James

Early November, 2003, Richmond Detectives were investigating a homicide at a DMV. Evidence suggested that the DMV crime scene was a dead-body dumpsite. Homicide Detectives contacted the Drug Enforcement Administration (DEA). City Detectives told the DEA that the murder, and the victim, were likely related to large scale drug activity, thus identifying the corpse as a person of interest to the Feds.

When DEA arrived at the murder scene, they were able to identify the deceased as one of their informants. For nearly a decade, a paid Jamaican known as Everette James (his tipster code name) was making a pretty good living turning in heavily armed crack dealers from Richmond to New England. DEA records indicated that Everette James' legal name was Anthony Novedo Rankine.

Everett James was the man who had been shot in the back of the head. Everett was the man whose hands and feet were bound by duct tape. Everette's blood, the carpet that he was wrapped in, and a handgun found nearby helped authorities establish that the home on Ammons Avenue in Henrico County, Virginia was the site of his murder.

The Drug Enforcement Administration quickly recognized that Everett had been dealing marijuana as a side hustle, simultaneously snitching on cocaine distributors while collecting checks from the DEA payroll. As the investigative dominoes started to fall in place, law enforcement realized that Everett was the man from the murder and missing person case in Chesterfield.

Federal and local investigators knew it was time to team up and compare notes.

Power of Music

Songs often reduce stress. Music can help heal a person of emotional and physical problems. Musical harmonies can solve gruesome murders. Wait, what does music have to do with homicide resolution? It turns out that rhythmic melodies and a little luck helped officers in metro Richmond solve a high-profile triple murder case.

Drug Enforcement Administration Supervisor Joe Dombrowski remembers standing in a Home Depot parking lot in Western Henrico County when he received a call for help from Chesterfield County officers who were working a drug related murder. Contemporaneously, a regional drug task force Detective also got a call, albeit from a concerned citizen. "The Jamaicans involved in the triple murder were heading out of town, but before they left, they wanted a tricked out stereo system," said Dombrowski.

The owner of a local automotive customization shop was friendly with some Henrico County police officers. This concerned citizen called a Detective friend, telling him that 7 Jamaicans were in the shop. The owner advised that the customer behavior, plus gut instinct, made him feel as if something wasn't right. The business owner provided personal identification information and a license number to the Detective.

The task force Detective used the information provided to query the DEA database. The customer information identified the questionable shopper as a Jamaican drug dealer. Uniform police officers were sent to the retail establishment to investigate. Dombrowski recalls, "There was something wrong with the cars registration, so we told marked units to hook them and bring them to us." It would propel wheels into motion for a murder investigation that would take detours, twists, and turns through several jurisdictions.

Interview and Interrogation

Investigators from multiple jurisdictions strongly suspected that the 7 Jamaicans found at the audio shop were somehow connected to the triple murder. "We interrogated suspects for hours, literally hours," said Dombrowski. We all came out, talked, we picked out what [who] we thought would be the weakest link. The team of investigators agreed on whom they would go at first." Intense grilling followed.

Dombrowski wanted to be able to charge all seven men with federal drug charges. Federal charges would provide significant motivation toward getting the detainees to roll on who committed the murders. The tactic worked. One investigative team got the youngest Jamaican to confess that he had driven to Richmond with about 150 pounds of pot to piece out in the Richmond area. "Once he admitted to the drug charge, we had em," exclaimed Dombrowski. He says he "Whipped out a legal pad and reverted to his old school ways, telling the suspect to write everything down."

Soon, the second of seven suspects would also confess to being involved in the narcotics business. Once the drug confessions were in the bag, investigators understood that they needed to strike again while the iron was hot. Chuck James, the local U.S. Attorney at the time, was brought onsite in case a prosecutorial deal became an option that needed to be put into play.

During one interrogation, Dombrowski stated that he "burst in the door" and said, "Where's the body? Tell me where the kids' body is or you're going to get the death penalty federally." The young man was crying. He was "devasted at the kidnapping of the kid [Marquis Jobes]. He [Jobes] was just there, wrong place, wrong time when they [killers] came in to take everybody down," said Joe Dombrowski. The confessor didn't know the geography of the city very well, but he volunteered to take investigators to where they dumped the body of 13-year-old Marquis Jobes.

Recovery of Marquis Jobes

With the cooperating witness in tow, investigators found their way to a large, big-box retail establishment on Midlothian Turnpike at Chippenham Parkway. The witness led them to a shallow creek behind the building, where Marquis Jobes' remains were found. It was the ending to an exhausting search that investigators had feared.

The innocent teenage boy, an honors student at Falling Creek Middle School, was snatched from his home as he played video games. Now he is dead simply because his family was involved with a Jamaican Drug Cartel. "We were all hoping that we would find the kid [Jobes] alive, but he saw it, saw the mother [get killed], and, he could recognize Bernard," said Dombrowski.

Bernard's Downfall

Six of the Jamaican drug dealers found at the audio installation shop told law enforcement that Richard Dwight Bernard had killed Anthony Rankine, Marquis Jobes, and Tasha Robinson. Each of the drug suspects independently "Flipped on him [Bernard], every one of them pled, nobody went to trial," said Dombrowski.

Why It Happened

Everett, the weed dealer who was moving thousands of pounds of marijuana along the East Coast corridor, tried to protect himself by being an informant for law enforcement. However, his biggest mistake was bringing in the wrong relative to help run his drug organization. Unfortunately for Everett, Richard Dwight Bernard was an ambitious, jealous uncle. Lower in the food chain, and wanting to be the boss, Uncle Richard had no problem taking out his nephew so that he could take his place. "Jealousy and money," Joe Dombrowski said.

Those who live by the sword, often die by the sword. An adult life of slinging rock for the feds and working as an undercover informant made the "Murder Mon" family vulnerable to violence. A triple murder investigation linked to organized crime, where luckily, investigators didn't miss a beat.

CHAPTER **14**

Valentine's Day Shooting Gallery

Richmond, Va. 2001, Steve Neal and Jon Burkett know the case well.

Home Invasion Robbery

Every year on February 14th, people honor one another by spending time together and sharing messages of love. Sadly, the ritual of expressing affection for family and friends didn't extend to one home in the Brookland Park area of North Richmond on the second Valentine's Day of the new millennium.

Around 10 pm., a young man named Lynwood Thrower confronted Matthias Washington on the front porch of a home in the 3100 block of Garland Avenue. Thrower demanded fifty dollars and drugs from Washington. When the robbery victim stated that he didn't have either money or drugs, court records indicate that Thrower said, "I'm going to come back with my boys, and you're going to be my next victim." Thrower left the scene in a four-door gray Cadillac.

He Came Back with the Boys

At 10:56 p.m., just as he had promised, Lynwood Thrower returned to the Garland Avenue address. With Thrower were Jamar Paxton,

William Sally (known as Orbit), and an unidentified fourth man. Thrower, wearing a bulletproof vest, was armed with an AK-47 style rifle. Court testimony indicated that Thrower directed Paxton, Sally, and the unnamed individual to go around to the back of the house.

Matthias Washington testified that he saw Thrower outside of the address. Rightfully fearing for his life, Washington ran inside and up the staircase, passing upper-level resident Adrian Harris. Washington exited through a top floor window and escaped by jumping off the porch roof. According to trial testimony, Thrower came inside the home, walked up the stairs and placed the muzzle of the high-capacity rifle between Harris' eyes.

Kayla Monique Brown

Melvin Brinkley and girlfriend Roberta Latham were residing on the first floor of the Garland Avenue multiplex. Brinkley was babysitting 23-month-old Kayla Brown. The couple and the child were asleep on a sofa. They were awakened when the back door of the house was kicked in, followed by gunshots. More details of the shootout and Kayla will be found in the *Story Behind the Story* segment that follows this report.

Lead Flying – More than 40 Rounds Fired

Brinkley heard rounds being fired from the rear of the residence. When he went to investigate, he saw three men standing in the kitchen doorway. Brinkley reportedly heard someone say, "Get the money, get the drugs." Additional gunfire erupted before the three men left through the back door. Brinkley told police that he was unable to identify the men because it was dark and the power source to the home had been cut off.

Brinkley and Latham testified that when the shooting started, they instinctively ran from the home. Brinkley said that he remembered that toddler Kayla Brown was sleeping on the couch. Brinkley indicated that when he went back into the apartment to get Kayla, he closed and locked the door. At almost the same time, Lynwood Thrower, who was now back out front, began firing the high-powered rifle into the downstairs portion of the residence. More than twenty spent cartridge cases were later recovered around the porch at the front of the house.

Melvin Brinkley was hit in the leg during the barrage of gunfire. His injuries were not considered life-threatening. Baby Kayla Monique Brown was killed instantly as a result of multiple gunshot wounds to her head. After spraying the home with gunfire, the shooters fled the scene in Lynwood Thrower's Cadillac.

Nearly twenty additional empty cartridge cases were recovered in the rear of the home. Analysis revealed that the spent cartridge cases at the rear of the home had come from at least two (2) different guns. The ammunition and blood found at the rear of the house would turn out to be crucial pieces of evidence for the prosecution.

MCV Hospital for Treatment

On the night of the murder, Jamar S. Paxton went to the Medical College of Virginia (MCV) Hospital Emergency room for treatment of a gunshot wound. Virginia State law mandates that Health Care Practitioners report non accidental gunshot injuries to law enforcement. All U.S. states have similar obligatory regulations. Virginia State Code regarding compulsory reporting is as follows:

Va. Code § 54.1-2967. *Any physician or other person who renders any medical aid or treatment to any person for any* *wound which such physician or other person knows or has reason to believe is a wound inflicted by a weapon specified in § 18.2-308 and which wound such physician or other person believes or has reason to believe was not self-inflicted shall as soon as practicable report such fact, including the wounded person's name and address, if known, to the sheriff or chief of police of the county or city in which treatment is rendered. Any person participating in the making of a report pursuant to this section or participating in a judicial proceeding resulting therefrom shall be immune from any civil liability in connection therewith, unless it is proved that such person acted in bad faith or with malicious intent.*

Reacting to the physician notification, Richmond Police Detectives responded to the Medical College of Virginia hospital to interview the injured Jamar Paxton. When police arrived, they found Lynwood Thrower and William Sally in the waiting room. A Detective saw Lynwood Thrower's Cadillac parked in the emergency room driveway of MCV. By this time, police were also at the Garland Avenue address investigating the shooting at the home. Putting two-and-two together, law enforcement strongly suspected that the three at the hospital were likely involved in the Northside shooting spree.

Investigation & Evidence

Jamar Paxton arrogantly denied any knowledge of the crime. He claimed he was leaving his cousin's house when he was accidentally shot in the foot, and that his cousin had dropped him off at the hospital. Paxton said that friends Orbit and Lynwood Thrower had just stopped by the emergency room to check on him. According to trial testimony, Jamar Paxton denied being on Garland Avenue when Brinkley and Kayla were shot, he denied being in Thrower's Cadillac that evening, and he denied shooting a gun on that particular night.

Gunshot residue tests (GSR) are often used by law enforcement to help determine if the subject of the testing has recently discharged a firearm. The tests are performed by swabbing the hands of the potential suspect. When tested, if the subject has recently fired a firearm, they should have particles of primer (expelled from a gun when discharged) on their hands. GSR tests were performed on Paxton, Sally, and Thrower. *All three had primer residue on their hands.*

At the Crime Scene

A forensics crime scene investigator was able to determine that multiple weapons had been used during the deadly Garland Ave. home invasion. The diameter and characteristics of the ejected cartridges from the front of the residence proved that they had been fired from a high caliber rifle.

Blood samples were collected from inside the back door of the downstairs apartment and on a piece of rubber hose found in the alleyway behind the house. Detectives were coordinating information from the Garland Avenue crime scene with the data they were obtaining at MCV Hospital.

Search of Thrower's Cadillac

Detectives at the hospital developed enough probable cause to search Lynwood Thrower's Cadillac. In the back seat of the vehicle they found blood, a bloody Timberland boot, a bottle of prescription drugs with Jamar Paxton's name on it, and a skullcap or "doo rag." DNA from blood at the crime scene, and in the automobile, would ultimately link Paxton to the crime.

Arrested

Police had more than enough evidence to charge William Aubrey Sally, 20, Lynwood Leroy Thrower, 21, and Jamar Shantae Paxton, 19, with murder, aggravated assault, and use of a firearm in the commission of a felony. All three were deposited into the City jail.

Paxton's Letter from Richmond City Jail

While incarcerated, Jamar Paxton and Lynwood Thrower exchanged letters through a jail trustee. The letters were intercepted by detention center staff and examined. Police learned that Paxton was attempting to set an alibi by telling Thrower how to testify at trial. Though not in its entirety, the following is an excerpt from one of Paxton's letters:

> "I didn't want to tell them I was anywhere near the house but I'm trying to help you. They have eye witnesses saying that me and Orbit was on the back porch the whole time then they heard me say oh shit and me and Orbit ran to the car. I can't say that I shot myself because they checked me for gun powder and I didn't have any on my hands. So, that won't work. Just tell them that me and Orbit was on the back porch and you went around the front. Me and Orbit will tell them that we didn't even see you with a gun.

> "You get what I'm saying? I'm not going to snitch on your ass or nothing like that. I will do whatever I can to help you as far as stretching the story but I can't tell them I did something that I didn't do and especially something that

DNA will prove I didn't do because that will cross me up. I got your back though. Everybody be chillin. I'll holla back."

A forensic document examiner compared the confiscated letters to known writings of Paxton and Thrower. The specialist testified that it was his expert conclusion that the seized letters had in fact been written by inmates Jamar Paxton and Lynwood Thrower.

Convicted and Incarcerated

When Lynwood Thrower learned that he was the man who fired the shots that killed Kayla Brown, his conscience ate at his soul. He admitted his involvement, telling investigators that he had a little girl the same age as Kayla, and he had to take responsibility for his actions. Part of that accountability would lead him to become a Commonwealth witness against Paxton and Salley.

As part of a plea bargain, Lynwood Leroy Thrower entered an *Alford Plea* to first-degree murder, use of a firearm during the commission of a murder, and attempted robbery. An Alford Plea allows a defendant to acknowledge that prosecutors have enough evidence to convict him, but falls short of an admission of guilt.

Thrower, Inmate # 1097685 at the Wallens Ridge State Prison, has a scheduled release date of 03/16/2055.

Jamar Paxton was convicted in a jury trial of first-degree murder, use of a firearm during the commission of a murder, maiming, attempted robbery, shooting into an occupied dwelling,

use of a firearm during the commission of a malicious wounding, and use of a firearm during the commission of an attempted robbery. Jamar Paxton, Inmate # 1121199 at the Sussex I State Prison, has a scheduled release date of 02/08/2069.

William Sally, Inmate # 1065344 at the Sussex II State Prison, was also convicted. He was released from prison in 2019 after serving eighteen-years.

Story Behind the Story

Powerful Pillowcase

Nineteen inches in width, and twenty-five inches long; standard measurement for a bedroom pillowcase. Millions lay their heads on them every evening for a good night's sleep. Nineteen-years-ago, life forever changed for all that witnessed the awful scene on Garland Avenue in Richmond, Virginia. Standing at the corner of Brookland Park Boulevard, the view looking into the bowels of the Northside was life altering. The value of holding your loved ones close was magnified.

Senseless Violence

Three gunmen, later identified as Lynwood Thrower, William Salley, and Jamar Paxton, purposely went to the Garland Avenue house that evening with mayhem on their minds. Upon arrival, the bad guys gave chase, surrounded the outside of the home, and opened fire as the target of the robbery fled into the residence. Thrower was searching the front yard, brandishing an AK-47 rifle while wearing a bulletproof vest.

Jamar Paxton and William Salley were around back. Paxton shot into the back door of the home with his gun while attempting to kick the door in. Paxton left a perfect shoe print on the back door and shot himself in the foot as he launched his leg towards the doorframe. Thrower opened fire out front, randomly spraying the facade of the house with high-powered rifle rounds. The reckless gunmen exhibited total disregard for the safety of innocents inside the home.

There was a Baby in the House

The streets were buzzing, rumblings that a sweet, innocent baby had been the victim of gun violence. A simple click of the record button on a DVCPRO camera would chronicle the event forevermore. Empathetic minds working the scene struggled to focus on the job at hand. Reporters and law enforcement universally affirm that crimes against children induce a different emotional response from witnesses.

Regardless of profession, mothers and fathers everywhere feel like they've taken a knife to the chest when a child is killed. Parents supportively feel the pain, nausea, and unsettling nature of the moment. Intellectual deliberation typically takes the observer to "What if this were my child?" Emotional trauma is amplified when the working professional has a child of nearly the same age or gender.

Working the Scene

A large Chevrolet Suburban with tinted windows delivered the Medical Examiner to the Garland Avenue scene. The finality of the presence of the Coroner walloped those nearby like a ton of bricks. As officials emerged from the vehicle, the vivid sound of a thud from shoes on the running board is something that can't soon be forgotten.

Next to arrive on scene was the body removal service. One specialist went to the rear of their SUV and swung the double doors open. Experienced witnesses on a scene like this would expect a metal gurney to be lowered out of the back of the vehicle. This time, the only thing detected was the repositioning of the gurney. The next thing that witnesses observed, was an arm reaching into a zipped body bag, pulling out a pillowcase. With only the pillowcase in hand, the well-dressed body removal specialist lifted the yellow crime scene tape and made his way towards the front door of the house.

Zooming in with the camera illuminated the consequences of AK-47 bullets that had ripped through the exterior siding and windows of the home. The visual made it appear as though the house had been constructed out of paper mâché instead of concrete and wood.

The midnight air of February, 2001, offered bitterly cold temperatures. Senses on high alert detected a change of sentiment as the three news professionals on-scene prepared for the "Money shot." The money shot is a piece of video that will stir the emotions of viewers at home as they watch the evening news. It was apparent to all the witnesses that something tragic was about to be revealed.

Ten-minutes of anticipation stretched into twenty. A few more minutes, then the clank of a doorknob and the click of a screen door. Out first was one of the well-dressed professionals from the medical examiner's office, holding the door for their colleague. Suddenly, the heartbreaking image surfaced. A toddler sized corpse wrapped in a pillowcase. A spot of blood about the size of a quarter could be seen on the front of that cotton casing.

23-Month-Old Kayla Monique Brown

Later, the public would learn that the small lifeless form in the pillowcase was a toddler named Kayla Monique Brown. Her young body had been pierced by AK-47 rounds that would slice through the front door like hot bread and shatter the top of her head. Kayla lived in the duplex style home, and was downstairs sleeping on a couch beside her bassinette. Melvin Brinkley also lived at the Garland Avenue address, and even though he was not related, was babysitting Brown that frosty evening.

A little girl's brain matter on the ceiling above a couch in a darkened living room, an image that retired Richmond Police Detective James Simmons says he can never forget. The night of Kayla Brown's death, Simmons had been enjoying a romantic dinner with his wife. You will recall that it was Valentine's Day, and certainly the thought of something as tragic as a young child dying by gunfire was the last thing on the Detective's mind.

What Could Have Been

Kayla Brown, if alive in the present day, would be 21-years old. If things had only been different; what if Kayla had been with her birth mother on that tragic night? What if her caretakers had been in a better living situation? What if the young, drug inspired, armed to the teeth ruffians hadn't been intent on robbing someone?

If Kayla had been in a different place at a different time; what would she look like today? Would she have made a magical mark on society? Would maturing into a young lady have allowed her to steer clear of the cycle of violence and drugs that engulfed the world where she laid nearly two-decades ago?

It is impossible to say what would've become of Kayla as a young woman; however, her premature death is something that witnesses will carry in their heart until their time is finished. The horror of the Kayla crime scene, and her tragic story, forever changed life perspective for countless individuals. Often, we wish things would've been different for Kayla. She is a stark reminder that life on earth is precious, and tomorrow is never promised.

The Grace of God

The horror of the evidence left at the crime scene has followed Detective Simmons into his retirement. Still fresh in his mind close to two decades later, Simmons said, "I'll tell you man, over the years I have to thank God that He allowed me to sleep at night, He didn't give me bad dreams, or you know, haunt me with this stuff. They say sometimes you are truly chosen for a job and the job don't choose you. There are some things that ordinary people couldn't deal with, so I guess it is truly grace."

Nine-years removed from his role as a Major Crimes Detective in the City of Richmond, Virginia, Simmons still crosses paths with parents and loved ones who have cases that are not solved. He tries connecting those families with cold case detectives in an effort to work on getting them some closure. "What can I tell those parents even though I'm no longer working, except hey, I'll check or I'll connect you with someone who can help," said Simmons.

Simmons says throughout his tenure as a homicide Detective, Kayla Brown's killing attached to his heart due to her age at time of death. It was her case and others that would remind the veteran officer to never let his love for his own son fall to the wayside. "I would come home and kiss [his son] and tell him I loved him every night, religiously," exclaimed Simmons. "In my years, I've sat across the table from pure evil and I've said if your ass ain't the closest thing to Satan, then I ain't going to meet him."

Readers of this story, as you raise your children or grandchildren, tell them the tale of Kayla Monique Brown. Maybe Kayla's shortened life story can help keep some impressionable young people from embarking on a path in life where their actions risk injury or death. Perhaps Kayla's legacy will be to prevent other young people from being carried out the door of their home in a pillowcase.

CHAPTER **15**

Grizzly Bear / Teddy Bear

DINWIDDIE, VA 2013, *Jon Burkett and Steve Neal*
know the case well.

March 7, 2013

Thirty minutes before he was scheduled to get off-work, a 40-year veteran Virginia State Trooper was shot and killed on Interstate I-85 near mile marker 45.

Master Trooper Junius Alvin Walker

At the time of his death, Badge # 802, was the most senior African-American officer at the Virginia State Police. Sixty-three (63) years-old, a member of the U.S. Army Reserves, he stood 6 feet 2 inches tall, and weighed well over 350-pounds.

"He was built like a grizzly bear, but he had the disposition of a teddy bear," said State Police Superintendent W. Steven Flaherty. At the memorial service,

Flaherty said that Walker had been a man of "Excellent character, and unshakeable integrity."

Gov. Bob McDonnell said that Trooper Walker "truly had the heart of a servant." A former State Police Superintendent eulogized the fallen hero as a "humble man, and a good listener, who rarely interrupted anyone and had a long fuse." Other speakers universally remembered Walker as a wonderful man, an exemplary trooper, and a man who would be greatly missed.

Trooper Walker, married father of two grown daughters, was known to go out of his way to be friendly. Assigned to Dinwiddie County, Virginia for 27-years, Walker had recently been honored by the Sutherland Ruritan Club for his years of dedicated work. A frequent lecturer at traffic safety seminars, Walker had talked privately about retiring. Nearly 3,000 people attended his memorial service at the Good Shepherd Baptist Church in Petersburg, Virginia.

The Crime

At approximately 1:30 p.m., a lone male was sitting in the driver's seat of a borrowed 2000 Lincoln LS automobile on the side of an Interstate highway just outside of Petersburg, Virginia. As he had done thousands of times previously, Trooper Walker eased his southbound squad car onto the shoulder of I-85 to check on what he thought was a disabled driver. When he pulled along the right side of the dark sedan, the suspect suddenly opened fire on the officer with a high-powered .308 caliber rifle.

Trooper Walker's Virginia State Police vehicle lurched forward, eventually coming to rest in the woods some 30-feet off the Interstate. A passing motorist called 911 to report that a State Trooper was in distress. Another caller said that he saw the police vehicle roll into the woods and into a ditch. This witness conveyed that he saw a man with a rifle aiming at the trooper's car and that a rear passenger window had been shot out.

A truck driver stopped his box truck along the highway when he saw the State Police vehicle in the woods. The driver of the truck exited his rig to investigate. As he was approaching the Trooper's vehicle, he could see the officer slumped over behind the wheel. Suddenly, a man with a rifle emerged from a crouched position. The trucker immediately turned away and retreated toward his rig. After climbing back into the cab, the truck driver heard three or four shots. At least two rounds struck the truck, one shattering the passenger window, and another that pierced the windshield in front of the driver's face.

Prior to any radio dispatch of Trooper Walker's predicament, a different Virginia State Police Trooper happened to be going by on his way home. As he came onto the scene, he saw Walker's vehicle in the woods, and he saw the suspect firing into Trooper Walker's police cruiser. This Trooper bailed out of his automobile and discharged suppression fire from his sidearm. He then retrieved his patrol rifle from his trunk. The Trooper and the suspect exchanged gunfire over the course of several minutes.

The suspect fired at least 29-rounds before he fled on foot into the woods. The suspect discarded clothing as he absconded. He also dropped his firearm and a magazine while attempting to escape. The heat from the engine of Trooper Walker's vehicle caused a brush fire underneath the squad car. Additional arriving officers were able to remove Trooper Walker from the burning vehicle. Sadly, he had been shot multiple times, and died from his injuries. More details of the shootout and the rescue attempt will be found in the *Story Behind the Story* segment that follows this report.

Arrest

As additional officers from multiple agencies began arriving, a mammoth manhunt got underway. Tracking dogs and a police airplane were called to the scene. Approximately 18-minutes into the search, the accused was found naked, hiding inside a Toyota Camry at Bishop's Towing on Boydton Plank Road. This location was approximately one-half mile from the shooting scene. Deputies with the Dinwiddie County Sheriff's Office took the subject into custody without incident as he screamed "Don't kill me."

The man in custody told State Police that he had smoked marijuana on the day of the shooting. Police found residue of the green leafy substance in the vehicle abandoned on the side of the Interstate highway.

Russell Ervin Brown lll, was charged with capital murder of a police officer, attempted capital murder of a second officer, and two counts of using a firearm in the commission of a felony. The 28-year-old Brown was taken to the Meherrin River Regional jail in Alberta, Virginia.

Suspect Background

The suspect in Trooper Walker's killing was a troubled individual who was leading a chaotic life. A Brown family member told a local news station that Brown was facing intense pressure over mounting child support, and the recent death of his mother. Court records show that Brown was more than $35,000 behind in child support payments, and was facing an upcoming trial for failure to comply with the court order.

At the time of the murder, Brown was an unemployed barber who didn't even have enough money for gas. He and a woman with whom he was living, had been given a nonpayment of rent eviction notice from the apartment that they shared.

In addition, at the time of the killing, Brown had no valid driver's license. Charges of driving without an operator's license and having an expired state registration sticker, stemmed from a traffic stop by a Virginia State trooper in August, 2012. The traffic stop by that trooper took place only seven months prior to the fatal encounter with Trooper Walker. Brown failed to appear for these charges and had his driver's license suspended indefinitely.

Russell Brown's grandmother told police that she had spoken to him often in the month leading up to the crime. At trial, she testified that Brown was talking about the Bible, and that he was not making much sense.

Physical Evidence

State police agents impounded the car Brown had been using. They obtained a search warrant that allowed them to thoroughly process the suspect vehicle. Four shell casings, glass fragments from the State Police car window, blood, and marijuana were among the items recovered. State Police investigators also recovered a partially empty Pepsi bottle, an electronic cigarette, swabs of red stains, swabs of black and green stains, and possible human tissue.

Police found a magazine containing two live rounds inside the car. A weapon was recovered in the woods not far from the shooting scene. Ballistic tests later determined that the recovered .308 caliber rifle was the weapon used to kill Walker.

Trial

Russell E. Brown's defense team initially entered an insanity plea for the defendant. The defense presented evidence that statements that Brown had made while in custody demonstrated that he was mentally unfit to stand trial. The defense also indicated that Brown had a fixation on religious symbolism, prophesy and a fatalistic belief in the upcoming end of the world that gave him delusions of grandeur, and a belief that his actions were part of a preordained mission from God.

Following much debate, A Dinwiddie County judge found Brown mentally incompetent, and thus unfit to stand trial. The judge ordered that Brown be sent to a state mental hospital for treatment in an effort to restore his competency. In March, 2015, Brown was ruled competent to stand trial and his mental health review was terminated.

In July, 2016, Brown was once again before a Dinwiddie County Court to face capital murder charges. The defense again entered a plea of insanity on his behalf. For those who may be unaware, states that accept insanity as a defense require that the burden of proof shifts to the defendant. In other words, the *defense must prove* that the defendant was insane at the time of offense. If an insanity defense succeeds, the accused may be found guilty but insane, and sentenced to a psychiatric institution rather than to prison.

At trial, two psychological experts testified that it was their opinion that Brown suffered from "bipolar disorder, experiencing bouts of both depression and mania, and that he suffered from psychotic episodes." However, prosecutors flatly rejected Brown's insanity defense and challenged the psychological assessment. They presented evidence that they believed would prove malice and aforethought regarding the defendant's actions.

In addition to physical evidence and witness testimony, the prosecution used Brown's own words against him. Trial testimony included that Brown told a Trooper "I saw the black officer's face, he looked like a dead man and he didn't know it." While in custody,

Brown further said, "As I saw the officer's face, I don't know what happened, I wasn't myself, I turned into a demon. I picked up my rifle and shot at him. The car kept on rolling in the grass. I got out after the car crashed, [and] I kept shooting him."

The prosecution also introduced statements by Brown in which he said in a calm and lucent tone, "I killed Walker" and "I'm fine with being executed." Further utterances included that Brown had told an interviewing trooper, "You will be the next to die" and that he "fully expects to have a needle stuck in my [Browns] arm."

On the eighteenth day of Brown's trial, following the presentation of 72 witnesses and 94 exhibits, the jury rejected the insanity defense and found Brown criminally culpable of all charges.

Conviction and Sentencing

Following a contentious three-week trial, Russell E. Brown lll, was found guilty of capital murder of a law enforcement officer, attempted capital murder of a different law enforcement officer, three counts of use of a firearm in the commission of a felony, and attempted murder of the truck driver.

The defense pleaded with the jury to spare Brown's life. The jury agreed, and condemned him to serve two life sentences plus 23-years in prison. Because of a Virginia law abolishing parole for all felonies committed after Jan. 1, 1995, theoretically he has no chance of being released.

In 2018, The Virginia Court of Appeals upheld all convictions. Russell Ervin Brown lll, is inmate # 1516821 at the Wallens Ridge State Prison.

Story Behind the Story

Valor

Virginia State Trooper Samuel Moss was a member of the State police sex offender investigative unit. He had spent most of his day checking to make sure that the lascivious wrongdoers were actually at the location of their registration. This particular day started at the field office not far from Petersburg, Virginia, where Moss would get to speak with Master Trooper Junius Walker one last time.

By early afternoon, Moss had finished his tour of duty. He was particular about having a full tank of gas and would often stop by the Department of Transportation refueling facility near Route 1 at the end of a shift. For some unknown reason, on March 7, Moss opted to skip the fill-up and head straight home.

Southbound on Interstate I-85, Trooper Moss finished a telephone conversation with his wife. Seconds later, Moss saw a Virginia State Police cruiser, lights activated, sitting off-road in the wood line. As he got closer, he noted a dark, four-door sedan and a white box truck parked on the shoulder nearby.

Unsure as to what was going on, Moss said he pulled his vehicle onto the shoulder. When he did, he saw a man with a long-gun. Suddenly, he realized, "Oh my gosh, he is shooting into the Trooper car." Trooper Moss had not heard any suspicious radio traffic. No 911 calls had been dispatched yet, and the lethally injured Trooper had been unable to call for help. Moss literally came upon the most dynamic, "hot" scene that law enforcement can encounter.

Trooper Moss immediately jumped out of his car and went to the right rear quarter panel for cover. He recalled that as he was bailing out of his car, the suspect turned toward him preparing to shoot. Trooper Moss gave the command of "State Police, Drop the Gun," and at the same time, laid down suppression fire with his sidearm. A fierce gunfight was underway. During the gun battle, Trooper Moss remembers thinking "I cannot believe that I just shot at somebody." It was a surreal moment for the veteran trooper.

Trooper Moss instantly recognized that his Sig Sauer .357 sidearm would not be the most effective weapon in this fight. After hitting the trunk release button, he retrieved his issued M4 carbine rifle from the trunk. With roughly 30-40 yards between them, a high-powered rifle skirmish lasted for approximately six minutes. During the encounter, Russell Brown even took cover inside the passenger cabin of Trooper Walker's cruiser.

Suspect Brown seemed to have some sense of tactics as he engaged in the firefight. At one point during the gun battle, Brown dove from the cruiser firing from a prone position on the ground. He also hid in the brush, darted out firing the weapon, and then retreated into the tree line for cover. As the firefight raged on, Trooper Moss stated that he remembered thinking "I'm going to get my head blown off at some point today, today is my day."

Trooper Moss thought lovingly of his wife and children. The father of six (6) knew he had to steel his emotions in order to get the job done. He was determined to stop the shooter; "I was convinced that he was killing this Trooper, and that he was trying to kill me. I know he was, there wasn't any doubt in what he was doing," Moss said.

As the gunfight lingered, Moss says he became more and more concerned for motorists who continued to whiz by even as bullets were being exchanged. Finally, a tractor trailer driver realized what was happening, and sealed off both lanes to keep motorist at a standstill. At one point, the truck driver yelled to Moss that the suspect had taken off in front of the trooper's car.

Eventually, Brown ceased firing and ran deeper into the woods. Trooper Moss could no longer see Brown, so he held his position, scanning the wood line for the threat. Backup officers arrived on the scene shortly thereafter. Moss maintained a cover position as responding officers planned the emergency rescue of Trooper Walker. What had been a routine day on the job was now every officer's worst nightmare.

Get There as Quick as Possible

The anguished cry of SHOTS FIRED across a police radio is the ultimate adrenaline jolt for law enforcement officers. It is understood that the proverbial shit has just hit the fan! On the afternoon of Trooper Walker's murder, Sgt. Marilyne Wilson's heart sank when she heard Trooper Moss's impassioned call for assistance. She immediately dropped what she was doing, and drove to help her co-worker. Knowing that she needed every RPM to get there as rapidly as practicable, she shut off her air conditioning and put the peddle to the meddle. Traveling twelve miles in just 6-minutes, she became the second officer on scene.

Trooper Bruce Carey had been in training on this day. He had just pulled into his driveway to go off-duty when he heard Trooper Moss' "Shots Fired" call over the radio. Without hesitation, the 17-year veteran put on his ballistic vest, left his home, and hightailed it toward the shooting site. A few minutes later, he and two Dinwiddie County, Virginia deputies arrived to augment the on-scene force.

Emergency Rescue

Though the shooting had stopped, the officers did not know the suspect's exact location. Did Brown flee through the woods, or was he hiding nearby, preparing to strike at them again? Within minutes of being on scene, the officers saw the grass beneath the State Police vehicle catch fire. "That's one of us," Sgt. Wilson thought. She said, "Despite what might happen, somehow we need to get him out [ASAP]." The heroes created a rescue plan on the spot.

Trooper Moss would provide cover with his rifle. Sergeant Wilson would use her vehicle as a shield. Crouched alongside the sheltering vehicle, Trooper Carey and Dinwiddie Sheriff Sergeant Jasen McClellan would carefully make their way toward the vehicle and the woods. Sgt. Wilson recalls that while driving, she was "hunkered down in the seat, pointing my rifle outside the passenger window." The cautious team moved slowly, trying to balance the need for expedience with safety. Hearts pounding, the team finally arrived within 7 – 8 feet of Trooper Walker's burning unit.

Even though they were concerned that the gunman could have them in his sights, Trooper Carey bravely broke from cover and ran toward Trooper Walker's flaming vehicle. "We didn't know if he was alive or if he had passed. We had to come up with something to get him out of the car. The man was my shift partner for 17-years, he had eaten at my dinner table many nights. I wanted to get to him, to help him," said Bruce Carey.

Due to his size, extricating the large man was very difficult. Sgt. Wilson joined the fearless struggle to remove their injured colleague from behind the wheel. The rescuers released the seatbelt and finally extracted the bloody Trooper from the car. "As we were taking him out of the car, fire was actually coming up thru the floorboard; you could see smoke and a little bit of flame," said Trooper Carey.

As the liberators were dragging the mountain of a man away from the vehicle, Walker's burning car burst into flames and exploded. Ammunition ignited in the trunk. The officer's thought that shots were once again being fired in their direction. After pulling Trooper Walker about 15 yards up an embankment, the heroes used a vehicle and formed an "L" shape to shield his body while waiting for the ambulance.

Trooper Walker was loaded into the ambulance and removed from the scene. However, the Troopers had to maintain their vigilance because the location of the shooter was still unknown. After the killer was in custody, sorrow engulfed the heroes. They knew that the man who was their friend, co-worker, and former training officer was fatally wounded.

A Lot Goes Through Your Mind

Law officers risk their lives daily. The ever-present danger is real, and officers understand that any minute of every day could be their last. It is not something that is dwelled upon, but the realism of the workplace condition does tend to make one circumspect. A strong sense of duty, and a robust desire to make a difference safeguarding the community motivates most officers to return day-after-day.

Trooper Moss, who has since been promoted to Sergeant, vividly recalls the moment that he first came face-to-face with the murderous suspect. After Brown was apprehended, Moss went to the arrest location to see if he could identify Brown as the shooter. Sgt. Moss remembers walking up to the car where Brown was being detained. He said, "This is the closest he and I ever got, just a piece of glass between us. I looked into his eyes, and he looked right back into my eyes, and I thought *this is the guy who just tried to kill me.*"

"The Lord was protecting me that day," said Sgt. Moss. He still marvels at the improbability of the encounter. "I was just on my way home; you look over to your right and see a guy shooting a State Trooper to death. You just don't see that," he said. Trooper Carey, who was promoted to Sergeant, said, "I never even thought about my own safety; I just reacted. Just did what I thought I had to do." "Sergeant Carey is the bravest guy I know," said Sam Moss.

Sgt. Wilson, who has since been promoted to Lieutenant, said that "No officer should have to see a fellow officer be shot like that; we did what we could." She went on to say that the incident has "made [her] appreciate life more than I did. God was with us that day, life is precious, live life to the fullest, [and] stop and think how blessed we are."

At Trooper Walker's memorial service, his widow engaged in a conversation with Lt. Wilson. "You know, what those troopers did [referring to the rescue extraction], allowed us to be here today," she said. "I wish that I could meet with them and talk with them." When Lt. Wilson indicated that she had been one of the rescuers, Mrs. Walker "gave me the biggest hug!" Lt. Wilson said that at that moment, she knew, "This is what it is about."

CHAPTER **16**

Allies Against Evil

Law Enforcement Leader

As a youth in Louisville, Kentucky, Steve Neal's young life revolved around basketball. He spent endless hours developing skills and polishing his ballplaying image. One sunny afternoon three friends called and asked him to join them in a pick-up game. Steve enthusiastically accepted the invitation and promptly climbed into the back seat of a car being driven by a roundball acquaintance.

Four teenagers in an automobile is often a recipe for disaster. As they became mobile, Steve had no idea that he was about to embark on an adventure that would change his view of the world, and affect him for the rest of his life. The driver of the vehicle produced a full-face Halloween mask. One of the friends suggested that they have some fun and see whom they could scare with the mask.

Wearing the mask, a baseball hat, and with a cigarette in his mouth, the driver of the vehicle began to approach various people, grunting and groaning at them. None of the immature boys ever considered that their playground was a strip-mall parking lot. A bank teller at a drive thru window of the local bank wasn't amused. Unbeknown to the pranksters, the bank teller called 911 and reported that four men with masks and guns had just tried to rob the bank.

Within minutes, countless police vehicles, with emergency equipment activated, converged on the *"suspect"* vehicle. More than ten officers surrounded the vehicle and aggressively confronted the teens. With their weapons deployed, some officers were yelling "Put your hands on the roof of the car." Other officers were screaming "Don't move, or I'll blow your brains out." After much confusion, the officers pulled the suspects out of the vehicle, slammed them over the trunk, handcuffed them behind the back, and forcefully threw them onto the ground.

Upon arrival at the police substation and subsequent interrogation, the police realized that the four youthful offenders never tried to rob a bank. However, local law enforcement was angry that foolish teens had endangered the public and wasted police time and resources. Steve was arrested and charged with one misdemeanor count of disorderly conduct. A magistrate set a ridiculously high bond to "punish" the fresh-faced eighteen-year-old. Incarceration followed in the city jail.

Just a few weeks into what we call adulthood, the teenager suddenly had his understanding of basic civil rights transformed. A law-abiding citizen who had been taught to respect the police, now possessed a shattered image of law enforcement integrity. Physical safety, filth, sexual propositioning, dignity, and psychological health all came to the forefront of Steve's existence as he confronted incarceration.

The court process that followed provided additional opportunities for personal growth. Against the advice of his attorney, Steve refused to accept a "guilty" plea bargain offered by the prosecutor.

Though he had no experience with the court system, he felt strongly that he was only guilty of riding in the back seat of a car. Threatened with the possibility of a 12-month jail sentence, Steve stood tenaciously by his lifelong philosophy of "*If you're right, you fight.*"

Against all probability, the prosecuting attorney abruptly and unexpectedly reversed course. The criminal charge against Steve was dismissed. This court victory reinforced a young man's belief that resistance against long odds and fighting for what you believe in is where justice can be found. The courage and pugnacity behind sticking to his principles allowed him to protect his criminal record.

The interval immediately following arrest, incarceration, and court process caused Steve to be very dissatisfied with the criminal justice system. He made a conscious decision to fashion success from adversity. His law enforcement career choice was a direct result of the realization that he could have enormous impact by joining the police business and influencing the actions of those in the system.

Steve brought a perspective to policing that most officers have never experienced. He quickly discovered that he had a passion and an aptitude for the business, especially investigating major felony cases such as homicide, robbery, rape, and child abuse. For many years, Steve trained recruit officers in the laws of arrest and the use of appropriate force. He taught and practiced leadership throughout his long and storied career.

Not only did he beat them, Steve Neal joined them! He is proud of his service, and gratified that his nearly 30-year career enabled him to make a consequential difference in the law enforcement landscape.

Crime Insider

Growing up as the middle child of 6, Jon struggled with getting the attention he thought he needed to be successful. He was hustling a buck by mowing neighbor's yards and writing a community newsletter that he distributed monthly.

Jon's life took a wayward turn at 14 when his dad called his mom and told her that he was through with their marriage. That fateful phone call took place on his sister's birthday. Jon remembers it like it was yesterday. Soon after, he started hanging around older teens in the neighborhood, and even though he was warned, Jon thought he was untouchable.

One crisp fall day, two older friends rolled down the driveway with a pick-up truck full of "things" they needed to store in the garage. Though he thought it was a little weird, Jon didn't second guess anything until the next day. Two police cruisers and an unmarked came down the driveway and went straight toward the garage. The guys that were supposedly "friends" had lied about the "things" they were storing. Jon found out that day that not only was he being charged for stolen goods, but also grand larceny. Police had received a phone call that Jon stole the stuff that was recovered on his property.

Luckily, the detectives and patrol officer knew in their hearts that Jon didn't do what was alleged. After further investigation, they pinned it on the two "friends" that came to use the garage as storage. After several brushes with the law, Jon's grandmother begged him to "get his shit straight." Jon loved playing high school basketball, but due to unacceptable grades his senior year, he was cut from the team.

During the last two years of high school, Jon worked at Wendy's restaurant on Hull Street in Midlothian, Virginia. While he liked earning a check, Jon knew that job wasn't a profession. As fate would have it, one night put Jon on track for a career. It was close to midnight when the drive-thru signal went, "beep." The order taker said, "Welcome to Wendy's – may I take your order please." That order was taken in what Jon now knows is the "broadcasters voice."

The woman chuckled and pulled around. Sliding the drive-thru window open, Jon heard the woman ask, "Were you the one on the mic." Upon replying with an embarrassing "yes," the woman said, "I'm Lisa McKay with local radio station Q94; have you ever thought about doing broadcasting? You have sort of a nice rasp in your voice." Jon laughed and said, "I haven't given it a whole lot of thought."

Days later…another sign. A buddy from high school called and said he had joined the Navy, and asked if Jon would be interested. Jon agreed to take the entrance (ASVAB) test. He scored really well in English and picked the job of journalism, knowing that the career field included broadcasting.

Off to Great Lakes, Illinois. Eighteen-years old, scared, and flying on a plane for the first time in his life. On the flight, Jon remembered the not so good days that brought him to the point of choosing this lifepath. No traditional graduate from high school, borrow money, and go to college. Jon had a strong desire to do it on his own.

He graduated bootcamp and went to Fort Meade to attend what was called "A" school at the Defense Information School. "Can't be so bad of a school, right? I mean, Wheel of Fortune's Pat Sajak graduated from there too." Due to failing Public Relations and having to take it over, his first set of orders were issued – La Maddalena Broadcast Detachment, Sardegna, Italy.

For a dude that had struggled in his teens, he was enjoying the golden horseshoe up his ass. Three years in the Mediterranean and it was time to come back home. He received orders again to come back to Fort Meade, but he knew that he wanted to start dabbling in civilian broadcast work. Jon began moonlighting at WBFF Fox 45 in Baltimore. Decision time would be a year later. Either extend his naval service or get out and try to land a job.

Weeks before making his decision, Jon submitted several resumes. WTVR CBS 6 in Richmond, Virginia, reached out to him within two days of submission. He has never looked back. Now in his 20th year at WTVR, Jon has witnessed and covered major stories, from standing in sideways rain during Hurricane Isabel to five of the sniper killings in the Central Virginia area. He comes into homes as the Crime Reporter, updating viewers about sad scenes across the Commonwealth. Some of those scenes you became intimately familiar with as you read **Bearing Witness to Evil.**

The Crime Reporter and the Lawman

Herodotus, the ancient Greek historian known as the "Father of History," famously said, *"Of all possessions, a friend is the most precious."*

Jon and Steve's work connection benefits from an exceptional bond, one embodied by both camaraderie and collegiality. Though they come from different generations, both were privileged to have parents who taught them how to be men that cherish family and hard work. Guided by steadfast principles, they each strive for excellence in all endeavors.

The Crime Reporter and the Lawman are passionate about their chosen vocations. Energized, focused, and driven from within, both men feel a compelling urge to solve a case, help a victim, protect a life, guide a child, or simply offer kindness to those who are hurting. Each man introspectively views his profession as very meaningful. Deep-rooted devotion to justice fires a strong sense of belonging for both Steve and Jon.

Interestingly, both law enforcement and the media need the byproduct of the other to fuel success. Law enforcement uses the media to tell their story, and to help with the apprehension of bad guys. The news business uses law enforcement to generate interest in their product, thus building their viewership. It is not always a match made in heaven.

Associations, affiliations, and connections are among the highest priority for both the Lawman and the Crime Reporter. In both professions, the most successful are easily able to expertly intermingle with the public. The finest in both businesses gain the trust and confidence of their patrons, even while enduring the worst of circumstances.

Jon and Steve became allies against evil for the first time in 2001. Their professional paths led them both to a homicide investigation in Chesterfield County, Virginia. As the Watch Commander, the accomplished senior officer was delivering the press briefing to the local media.

Steve was immediately impressed with the young fellow who set up the CBS 6 camera. The questions he posed were relevant, logical, and right on point. It was obvious that the self-assured, youthful newsman was both prepared and poised. The internal confidence commingling with recognizable professionalism caught the veteran lawman's interest.

The wise amongst us understand that two individuals negotiate the boundaries of a robust relationship. Trust is the bond that enables successful police-media relations. Jon is a master at building trust. His word is binding, and Steve knew with 100% confidence that Jon would never betray that confidentiality.

Since that first fateful encounter, Steve and Jon have collaborated on many high-profile assignments. Jon often relies on Steve to be his expert crime analyst when it comes to producing crime and cold case stories for local news programming. Steve offers insight and analysis that gets straight to the point and turns out to be "dead on" 99.9 percent of the time.

Charles Darwin, the 19th century naturalist and biologist known for his theory of evolution, once said that *"A man's friendships are one of the best measures of his worth."* Shared work values and skills facilitate a deep respect between Steve and Jon that has blossomed into a great friendship. The Crime Reporter and the Lawman are fortunate to enjoy a bond that overflows with personal and professional wealth.

CHAPTER 17

Culmination – Good Vs. Evil

Throughout history there has been spirited debate about whether mankind is intrinsically good or inherently evil. Are people innately peaceful and pure? Followers of this ideology tend to believe that we are corrupted by the influences of society. Or, are individuals naturally cruel and sinister? Supporters of this philosophy contend that societal regulations help to improve upon the corrupt human disposition. Whatever our inborn proclivities, it seems apparent that human beings are a concoction of both positive and negative virtues.

Bearing Witness to Evil epitomizes the dichotomy between that which is righteous and that which is depraved. Our world can be a zany place, simultaneously and instantaneously alternating between profound euphoria and excruciating agony. The humanness of mankind is the story of a complicated conglomerate of contradictions, paradoxes, antonyms, enigmas, and oxymorons. Free will and choice, are navigational beacons that give us wide ranging control over our domain.

Bearing Witness – Fighting for justice for those who are grieving embodies the tenderhearted act of witnessing. Compassionately working on behalf of someone in distress confers reverence, safety, and comfort to survivors. While helping co-victims deal with suffering, honor and healing is bestowed upon victims, survivors, and their loved ones. Support of the incapacitated reveals our respect toward the living and the dead. Bearing Witness allows us to employ a belief system that is focused on providing support in coordination with inhibiting the wicked.

Evil – means something contrasting with that described as being virtuous. Evil is something which is immoral, sinful, diabolical, and repugnant. Corrupt wrongdoers demonstrate an appalling lack of concern, heinously putting their needs before others. The depraved, loathsome, sinister acts featured in this book can be described as morally evil. The villainous offenders who dominate our stories personify evil, and illuminate the worst wickedness imaginable. Their insidious choices drove despicable and repulsive destruction. These evildoers misapplied mankind's power to act.

Our Choices – As a Lawman and a Crime Reporter, our jobs frequently place us in the position of ***Bearing Witness to Evil*** while on the job. We pledge to combat sorrow and atrocity by:

- Serving others
- Seeking justice for those who have been harmed
- Being compassionate
- Treating everyone with dignity and respect
- Representing those who are suffering
- Challenging injustice
- Fighting against wickedness so that good may result

As Jon and Steve wage war against criminal decadence, the following quotes from the Bible seem a perfect fit; "As for us, we can't stop speaking about what we have seen and heard" (KJV ACTS 4:20). "The righteous care about justice for the poor, but the wicked have no such concern" (KJV Proverbs 29:7). "When justice is done, it brings joy to the righteous, but terror to evildoers" (KJV Proverbs 21:15).

Participating in an esteemed altruistic endeavor may well provide the path to self-actualization. Genuine selflessness in the service of others leads to personal happiness. We leave each person reading this book with an individualistic challenge. Your task is to seek, and find, your distinctive benevolent niche. Once you decide how you can *Bear Witness*, serve others with great passion! Few things in life will be as rewarding.

Steve Neal – Is highly respected by those with whom he has served. His distinguished 29-year law enforcement career includes many awards and commendations. He is proud of his reputation as a "cop's cop," a leader who placed the welfare of those under his command as a top priority. Well known as a man of strong values, straight talk, and true to his word, he has been a mentor and coach to many co-workers.

Steve was the architect of Public Safety University. PSU was an educational partnership between the public safety community and the University of Richmond. Under his guidance as Program Director, 233 public safety officers from throughout the State of Virginia obtained Bachelor and/or Master's degrees through the PSU program.

Co-founder and partner of the Leatherman and Neal public safety consulting team, Steve enjoys providing leadership training for peace officers. In addition to his consultancy, he works as a media contributor furnishing expert law enforcement analysis, consultation, and crime commentary for television broadcasters. Steve has appeared as a law enforcement authority on the nationally syndicated television show *For My Man*.

Steve Neal is the author of the broadly praised leadership book, **Toxic Boss Blues**. He has written several articles that have been published online by *Law Enforcement Today, Law Officer, and Police One* magazines.

Jon Burkett - Seven days a week –morning, noon, and night, CBS 6 reporter Jon Burkett is always on the job: covering breaking news, working his sources, and getting exclusive details and interviews. Jon enlisted in the Navy after graduating from high school in 1995. He served five years and was bitten by the journalism bug while working for the American Forces Network, the broadcast service of the U.S. military.

After spending time overseas, Jon returned to the States, and was able to get a part- time job as a photojournalist at WBFF, Fox affiliate in Baltimore. He loved the news business, but didn't have a lot of down time. "I worked 7 a.m. to 4 p.m. for the Navy, and then 5 p.m. to 11 p.m. for the station," Jon said. In Baltimore, Jon became a skilled photojournalist. But the Chesterfield native wanted to come home, and that happened about the time he left the service, when a job became available at CBS 6. Jon started as a photographer, shooting and editing video for newscasts and reporters. A natural storyteller, he was soon given the chance to report on his own. Two decades later, he has become the backbone of the CBS 6 newsroom.

Despite his many accomplishments, Jon had one goal that for years went unfulfilled. He wanted to graduate from college. In 2009, he turned his attention towards obtaining a degree, and started taking classes online. Because of his military service, Jon had the GI Bill to help him cover the cost of tuition. But he waited too long to use it, and it expired in 2010, 10 years after he was discharged. "I basically left $23,000 on the table," Jon said.

Two years later, his fortunes improved. "I'm listening to a Redskins Monday Night Football game, and Jim Gray is interviewing Larry Fitzgerald," Jon said. "At the end, Fitzgerald starts talking about his 'Focus to the Finish' scholarship." According to the University of Phoenix website, Fitzgerald, a Pro Bowl wide receiver for the Arizona Cardinals, created the scholarship for people who have, for various reasons, had to put the dream of getting a college degree on hold. Jon applied, and wrote a letter telling his story. "Four months later, right after the new year [2015], I got a letter saying I was one of 49 chosen," Jon said. "The rest is history.

Jon Burkett is the Crime Insider. He can be seen on WTVR TV-6 in Richmond, VA, and on several crime series that air on TV-One and Investigative Discovery.

Works Cited

n.d.

Amnesty International Global Report. 2019. *Death Sentences and Executions 2018.* Accessed October 4, 2020. https://www.amnesty.org/download/Documents/ACT5098702019ENGLISH.PDF.

Baker, David. 2019. *The world's first killer to be caught by his own DNA - a breakthrough that changed policing forever.* October 9. https://www.telegraph.co.uk/men/thinking-man/cracked-serial-murder-case-ushered-new-era-dna-policing/.

Blair, Peter. 2015. *Is a confession alone enough to convict a defendent.* November 6. https://www.blairdefense.com/is-a-confession-alone-enough-to-convict-a-defendant/.

Cormier, Lisa CalandroDennis J. ReederKaren. 2005. January 6. https://www.forensicmag.com/article/2005/01/evolution-dna-evidence-crime-solving-judicial-and-legislative-history.

Dundon, Rian. 2018. *Timeline.* Feb 23. Accessed April 20, 2020. https://timeline.com/rainy-bethea-last-public-execution-in-america-lischia-edwards-6f035f61c229.

Edward W.Murray. 1992. *Law Resource.* October 28. https://law.resource.org/pub/us/case/reporter/F3/005/5.F3d.758.92-4006.html.

2019. *FBI Services.* October 12. https://www.fbi.gov/services/laboratory/biometric-analysis/codis/codis-and-ndis-fact-sheet.

Foster, Richard. 2018. *12 On Your Side.* May 22. Accessed October 12, 2019. https://www.nbc12.com/story/38252654/podcast-to-reveal-never-before-heard-details-in-hunt-for-south-side-strangler/.

Frost, Natasha. 2018. *History channel.* August 24. Accessed Feb 22, 2020. https://www.history.com/news/death-penalty-jamestown-virginia-colony.

Fuchs, Erin. 2013. *Why America Gives Inmates Elaborate Meals Right Before Killing Them.* Sept 21. Accessed May 28, 2020. https://www.businessinsider.com/why-do-death-row-inmates-get-last-meals-2013-9.

Grillo, Ioan. 2014. *Combatting Terrorism Center.* January. Accessed September 6, 2020. https://ctc.usma.edu/jamaican-organized-crime-after-the-fall-of-dudus-coke/.

History.com. 2009. *History.* Nov. 16. Accessed April 16, 2020. https://www.history.com/this-day-in-history/300-santee-sioux-sentenced-to-hang-in-minnesota.

Innocence Project. 2008. *David Vasquez marks 19 years of freedom.* January 4. https://www.innocenceproject.org/david-vasquez-marks-19-years-of-freedom/.

Johnson, Robert. 2014. *Death Row Confinement and the Meaning of Last Words* . February 17. Accessed May 28, 2020. file:///C:/Users/Steve/Downloads/laws-03-00141-v2.pdf.

LesCault, Russ. 2012. *The History of Chesterfield Courthouse.* Accessed April 16, 2020. file:///C:/Users/Steve/Downloads/The+History+of+Chesterfield+Courthouse%20(4).pdf.

May, Mary. 2019. *Harvard Science in the News.* Accessed October 13, 2019. http://sitn.hms.harvard.edu/flash/2018/next-generation-forensics-changing-role-dna-plays-justice-system/.

Myatt, Mike. 2012. "Leadership -Why Yes is a Better Answer Than No." *Forbes.*

Namie, Gary. 2011. *The Bully at Work.*

Nasaw, Daniel. 2011. *BBC News.* September 11. Accessed May 28, 2020. https://www.bbc.com/news/magazine-15040658.

National District Attorney Association. n.d. *DNA Forensics.* Accessed October 13, 2019. http://www.dnaforensics.com/familialsearches.aspx.

1994. *New York Times.* April 29. https://www.nytimes.com/1994/04/29/us/in-a-first-man-convicted-on-dna-is-executed.html.

Podcast, Richard Foster. 2018. *12 On Your Side.* May 22. https://www.nbc12.com/story/38252654/podcast-to-reveal-never-before-heard-details-in-hunt-for-south-side-strangler/.

Ruane, Michael E. 2015. *Washington Post.* July 4. Accessed April 21, 2020. https://www.washingtonpost.com/local/four-people-were-hanged-for-lincolns-assassination--and-it-was-caught-on-camera/2015/07/03/377614d4-1905-11e5-ab92-c75ae6ab94b5_story.html.

Ryan, Perry. 2001. *NPR.* May 1. Accessed October 4, 2020. https://legacy.npr.org/programs/morning/features/2001/apr/010430.execution.html.

Selles, Theo. 2012. *How to Deal with Liars at Work.* Accessed April 23, 2012. www.hubpages.com.

Uenuma, Francine. 2018. December 5. https://www.smithsonianmag.com/history/first-case-where-fingerprints-were-used-evidence-180970883/.

UNODC. 2005. *From the United Nations Office on Drugs and Crime (UNODC) Homicide Statistics.* Accessed September 6, 2020. https://www.unodc.org/unodc/en/data-and-analysis/statistics.html.

Volsky, George. 1987. *New York Times.* July 19. Accessed September 6, 2020. https://www.nytimes.com/1987/07/19/us/jamaican-drug-gangs-thriving-in-us-cities.html.